Cost Sharing in Public Higher Education Institutions in Ethiopia with Special Emphasis on Addis Ababa and Adama Universities

Wanna Leka
&
Desalegn Chalchisa

FSS Research Report No. 8

Forum for Social Studies (FSS)
Addis Ababa

© 2012 by the authors and Forum for Social Studies (FSS)

All rights reserved.

Printed in Addis Ababa

Typesetting & Layouts: Konjit Belete

ISBN: 978- 99944-50-45-9

Forum for Social Studies (FSS)
P.O. Box 25864 code 1000
Addis Ababa, Ethiopia
Email: fss@ethionet.et
Web: www.fssethiopia.org.et

This Research Report was published with a core grant from the Civil Society Support Program (CSSP).

Table of Contents

	Page
List of Acronyms	v
List of Tables	vi
Abstract	viii
Chapter 1: Introduction	1
1.1. Background of the study	1
1.2. General objective of the study	8
1.3. Basic research questions	9
1.4. Significance of the study	10
1.5. Delimitations	10
1.6. Limitations of the Study	10
Chapter 2: Review of Related Literature	11
2.1. The concept of Cost sharing	11
2.2. Rationale for cost sharing	13
2.3. Tuition fees setting Policies in HEIs	14
2.4. Types of cost sharing policies in HEIs	17
2.5. The financial significance of tuition fees	22
2.6. Cost sharing recovery in HEIs	24
2.7. Perceptions toward cost sharing policies	30
2.8. Cost sharing trends in Public HEIs	31
Chapter 3: Methods of the Study	33
3.1. Design of the Study	33
3.2. Participants	33
3.3. Instruments	35
3.4. Procedures	35

3. 5.	Methods of Data Analysis	36
Chapter 4: Data Presentation and Analysis		**37**
4. 1.	Profile of respondents	37
4. 2.	Impact of cost sharing on service provisions	44
4. 3.	Qualitative Data Analysis	57
Chapter 5: Summary and Recommendations		**63**
5. 1.	Summary	63
5. 2.	Recommendations	64
References		67
Annex		73

List of Acronyms

AAU	Addis Ababa University
AU	Adama University
COP	Cut Off Point
CSA	Central Statistics Authority
ERCA	Ethiopian Revenue and custom Authority
ESDP	Education Sector Development Program
ETP	Education and Training Policy
FBE	Faculty of Business and Economics
FDRE	Federal Democratic Republic of Ethiopia
FSS	Forum for Social Studies
GDP	Gross Domestic Product
GER	Gross Enrolment Ratio
GET	Ghana Education Trust Fund
HEI	Higher Education Institutions
HELB	Education Loan Board
HICES	Household Income Consumption and Expenditure Survey
JAB	Joint Admissions Board
MA/MSc	Master of Arts/Master of Sciences
MDG	Millennium Development Goals
MOE	Ministry of Education
PASDEP	Plan for Accelerated and Sustained Development to End Poverty
PES	Private Entry Scheme
PUJAB	Public Universities Joint Admissions Board
SES	Socio-economic Status
SFAR	Student Financing Agency for Rwanda
SSNIT	Social Security and National Insurance Trust
TGE	Transitional Government of Ethiopia
UACE	Uganda Advanced Certificate of Education Examination
UEE	University Entrance Examinations
UK	United Kingdom
UPE	Universal Primary Education
US	United States
USA	United States of America
USD	United States Dollar

List of Tables

Table	Title	Page
Table 1.	Trend of students' enrolment in institutions of higher education in regular program and budget allocation (2003/04-2008/09)	8
Table 2.	Worldwide Types of Public Tuition Fee Policies	17
Table 3.	Types of tuition fee policies in Africa	22
Table 4.	Financial significance of tuition fees	23
Table 5.	Population and sample of the study	34
Table 6.	Number of Respondents from the Addis Ababa and Adama universities	37
Table 7.	Sex Composition of students and instructors	38
Table 8.	Distribution of Students and instructors by faculty/college	39
Table 9.	Educational qualification and academic rank of instructors	40
Table 10.	Types of services the students get as part of their cost sharing scheme	40
Table 11	Students' fathers and mothers educational level	41
Table 12.	Students' fathers and mothers occupation	42
Table 13.	Geographical location where students completed their secondary preparatory education	43
Table 14.	Expected cost recovery from Addis Ababa University graduates	45
Table 15.	Expected cost recovery from Adama University graduates	45
Table 16.	The extent cost sharing brought impact on teaching and learning by making facilities available	47
Table 17.	Expected qualities of facilities/services as the result of cost sharing scheme	48
Table 18.	Extent of the quality of services students expected as a result of cost sharing scheme	49

Table 19.	Extent of the quality of services students currently getting from their universities	50
Table 20	Services rated as high or low by cost sharing students from Addis Ababa and Adama universities	51
Table 21.	Students rating of the services they get currently from their universities considering what they will pay as a graduate tax	51
Table 22.	Graduates from Public Higher Education Institutions and estimated cost recovery (2003/04-2008/09.	52
Table 23.	Graduates and expected revenue to be collected by universities (2005/06 to 2009/10)	53
Table 24.	A Brief summary of basic facts related to cost-sharing scheme	53
Table 25.	Students boarding and food fees from 2005/06-2009/10	54
Table 26.	Cost sharing fees by field of study at Addis Ababa University (2009/10)	55
Table 27.	Cost sharing fees by field of study at Adama University (2009/10)	56

Abstract

The main purpose of this study was to investigate the impact of cost sharing scheme in enhancing revenue generation in public higher education in Ethiopia in order to improve the quality of the teaching and learning environment. Furthermore, the study has attempted to assess problems/challenges experienced by students as well as other government bodies related to cost sharing scheme. To this effect, both quantitative and qualitative research approaches were used. The participants for the study were students and instructors from Addis Ababa and Adama universities. A total of 1048 students and 123 instructors completed and returned questionnaires. To obtain qualitative data interviews were conducted with selected graduates from the two universities who went through the cost sharing scheme, the offices responsible for cost sharing at Addis Ababa University, the Ethiopian Revenues and Customs Authority as well as the Ministry of Education. Appropriate statistical tools were used for data analysis.

The finding of the study revealed that at the undergraduate level all students from different socio-economic backgrounds enter into an agreement for cost sharing. Students pay their cost of boarding, food and medicine and share 15% of the tuition fee. The tuition fee includes the cost incurred on instruction as well as on other expenses except boarding, food and medicine. Beneficiaries either pay their cost sharing in terms of services or upfront payment or a 10% graduate tax which is considered as high as compared with many African countries. Students get different kind of services as part of their cost-sharing scheme. The majority of the students get boarding and food services. Few students use food and boarding services. Students who opted either for only food or boarding accumulate less debt at the end of their college education than those who use both food and boarding services. Most students in both universities had either high or moderate expectations concerning the services when they joined these universities. However, most of the students rated the quality of various services they get as low compared with their expectations. Furthermore, it was also found that the government does not re-channel the collected revenues from the graduates to their respective institutions to augment yearly allocated budgets. Hence, it is recommended that concerned government bodies should tackle the problems associated with cost sharing in HEIs.

Cost Sharing in Public Higher Education Institutions in Ethiopia with Special Emphasis on Addis Ababa and Adama Universities

1. Introduction

1.1. Background of the study

The implementation of cost-sharing scheme in public higher education institutions (HEIs) in Ethiopia is a recent phenomenon as compared to some other East African countries: in Kenya in 1991 (Chacha, 2002 & Mwinzi, 2002), Uganda in 1990 (Mayanja, 1996), and in Tanzania in 1961 (Mpiza, 2007). Since the introduction of cost sharing policy in 2003/04 few studies were conducted in Ethiopia. The study by World Bank (2004) on higher education development in Ethiopia projected that by the year 2020 the share for higher education in total education spending would be some 4 to 5 percentage points lower with cost-sharing than without. Studies by Teshome (2003, 2007) detailed out the rationale for cost sharing and the appropriateness of graduate tax in recovering cost sharing. Abdena (2005) studied the attitude of HEIs students toward cost sharing in the Oromia Regional State. Cost sharing in Ethiopia was also included in the World Bank (2010) study of financing higher education. However, the implementation of cost sharing and the challenges associated with it have not been studied in detail.

Before going into the details of cost sharing in public institutions of higher learning, a brief profile of the country with special emphasis on the educational system seems mandatory. Ethiopia is a heterogeneous society with a population close to 82 million (UN, 2009) out of which 50.1% are males and 49.9% are females. 55% of the population is below the age of 20. Close to 85% of the population and 90% of the poor live in rural areas and most of them earn their living from rain-fed agriculture, which constitutes 52% of the country's GDP. Only 33% of the population is literate. With this record, it is considered as one of the poorest countries in the world with a per capita of USD 220 in 2008 (MOE, 2010).

Thus, one of the major development challenges for Ethiopia is to eliminate absolute poverty. According to the government's Plan for Accelerated and Sustained Development to End Poverty (PASDEP, 2005/6 – 2009/10), it was estimated that the country has to raise its economic growth to 8% annually to achieve the Millennium Development Goals (MDGs).

The government sees education and training as an important factor in the process of human resource development in order to break the vicious cycle of poverty that the country has been entangled in. According to Sodhi (1984), the contribution of education to the process of development of human resources has three major components: (a) in terms of economics, it may be described as the accumulation of human capital and its effective investments in the development of an economy, (b) in political terms, human resources development prepares for adult participation in political processes, particularly as citizens in a democracy, (c) from the social and cultural points, the development of human resources helps people to lead a happy life. In short, the process of human resource development unlocks the door to modernization.

Cognizant of these facts, the current government promulgated a number of social and economic policies since it took power in 1991. One of these policies is the Education and Training Policy (ETP) that came into effect as of 1994. In reference to higher education the ETP (TGE, 1994, p. 15) stated, "Higher education at diploma, first degree and graduate levels, will be research oriented, enabling students become problem-solving professional leaders in their fields of study and in overall societal needs".

In order to give legal framework for higher education institutions, the government has put into effect the Higher Education Proclamation No. 650/2009. According to the proclamation, the stated objectives of higher education are to (FDRE, 2009, p. 4979):

1. prepare knowledgeable, skilled, and attitudinally mature graduates with demand-based proportional balance of fields and disciplines so that the country shall become internationally competitive;
2. promote and enhance research focusing on knowledge and technology transfer consistent with country's priority needs;
3. ensure that education and research promote freedom of expression based on reason and rational discourse and are free from biases and prejudices;
4. design and provide community and consultancy services that shall cater to the developmental needs of the country;
5. ensure institutional autonomy with accountability;
6. ensure the participation of key stakeholders in the governance of institutions;

7. promote and uphold justice; fairness, and rule of law in institutional life;
8. promote democratic culture and uphold multicultural community life;
9. ensure fairness in the distribution of public institutions and expand access on the basis of need and equity.

According to Bolalag (2004), higher education plays a key role in the economic and social development of any nation. This is particularly the case in today's globalized, information and knowledge-based economy. No country can expect to successfully integrate in, and benefit from this 21st century without a well-educated workforce. Furthermore, higher education institutions are (a) expected to train the professionals and political leaders needed in various public and parastatal organizations bestowed also with the responsibility of shaping national development (Mugabushaka, Teichler & Schomburg 2003, p. 58). These mandates emanate from the fact that higher education institutions are often the only national institutions with skills, the equipment, and the mandate to generate new understanding through research. University roles in research, evaluation, information transfer, and technology development are therefore critical to national social progress and economic growth (Association of African Universities, 1997).

It is through quality tertiary level education that competent professionals who can play different roles to enhance the country's economic development could be trained. Many governments and writers have echoed the significance of higher education. Reflecting this reality, Bloom et al. (2005, p. 16) stated that:

> *Higher education can lead to economic growth through both private and public channels. The private benefits for individuals ... include better employment prospects, higher salaries, and a greater ability to save and invest. These benefits may result in better health and improved quality of life, thus setting off a various spiral in which life expectancy improvements enable individuals to work more productively over a longer time further boosting lifetime earnings. In a knowledge economy, tertiary education can help economies keep up or catch up with more technologically advanced societies".*

Aware of this reality, Ethiopia has embarked on the process of expanding education throughout the country at primary, secondary as well as at tertiary levels, especially after the government issued the Education and Training Policy (ETP) of 1994. In 2008/09 there were 23 government higher education institutions in Ethiopia enrolling a total of 263, 953 students at undergraduate and postgraduate levels (MoE 2010). However, according to Education Sector Development Program (ESDP) III (MoE, 2005) which covers the period from 2005/06 - 2010/2011, Ethiopia's tertiary level gross enrolment ratio (GER) stands at 1.5%. This GER is still low even compared to the Sub-Saharan standard, which is 5% (Materu, 2006). The student population per 100,000 in habitants is estimated to be only about 125-150 (Materu, 2006). In order to address this low enrolment rate at the tertiary level the government of Ethiopia in its Education Sector Development Program III (ESDP III) (MoE, 2005) pointed out that: the overall strategy concerning tertiary level education is to provide good quality higher education to a large number of students equitably but based on merit. This is mainly to meet the demand from the economy that is expected to grow steadily and will require large number of degree level graduates in different fields.

The demand for skilled professionals by the economy has been highlighted in a survey by Central Statistics Authority (CSA, 2010) on urban employment/ unemployment covering fifteen selected major towns with a population of 100,000 and above including regional capitals indicated that among the employed population in these cities, people working as professionals (people with tertiary level education) accounted for only 16%. This indicates that the country faces shortage of professionals, at the same time graduate unemployment is a growing problem.

On the other hand, Ethiopia has committed itself also to achieve Universal Primary Education (UPE) by the year 2015. In order to achieve UPE by the aforementioned time and also pull itself out of poverty, education and training have become some of the main focus areas of the government. After the enactment of the ETP (TGE, 1994), Ethiopia has also embarked on the expansion of higher education. According to ESDP III 2005/2006 - 2010/2011 (MOE, 2005), the tertiary level education expansion is a response to the anticipated skilled labour market demand and also as per the national development priorities However, as a developing country, Ethiopia has limited resources and cannot finance adequately all sectors of education.

Higher education is a very expensive endeavour. Available figures from the Ministry of Education indicate that the estimated recurrent spending per pupil (2007/08) at primary level for grades 1-8, for secondary level and for tertiary level were Birr 205, 455 and 6,646 respectively (MoE, 2008). This means that the cost of training a higher education student can train 32 primary or 22 secondary level students.

Todaro & Smith (2012) indicated that education has both social and private rates of return. In simple terms, the social rate of return is the benefit (direct/indirect) that the society gains as a whole. The private rate of return is the benefit that the individual gains after completing a certain level of education/training. Comparatively speaking, it was estimated that the social benefit of primary education is greater than that of tertiary level education. However, the private rate of return of higher education is estimated to be greater than that of primary level of education

Bloom, et.al (2005), Bishop (1989), Marcucci & Johnstone (2007) indicated that: (1) since higher education is expensive by its nature as compared with primary or secondary level of education countries having limited resources cannot meet all the demands of higher education; (2) It is believed that the future earnings of graduates of higher education will be high and therefore it is the beneficiaries that should cover most of the private educational costs; and (3) higher education, especially in developing countries, is more accessible to those students who come from relatively well-to-do families and from the urban areas. Thus, the equity/egalitarian argument states that the rural poor should not subsidize the education of the urban rich (Todaro, 1985).

In the Ethiopian context, 85% of the people and 90% of the poor live in rural areas (World Bank, 2008). Furthermore, 78% of all Ethiopians live on less than USD 2 per day (World Population Data Sheet, 2010).

In reference to the relation between socio-economic status and tertiary level education, Bishop (1989) indicated that:

> *The most deep-rooted and wide and widespread inequalities in education, especially in higher education, in both developing and developed countries are those arising from socio-economic status. ... children of parents who are high on the educational, occupational and social scale have far better statistical chance of getting into a good secondary school and from there into one of the better or best colleges or universities than equally bright children of ordinary workers or farmers (p. 43-44).*

According to Sawyerr (2004), students attending institutions of higher learning in African countries, such as Mozambique, Uganda, Senegal, etc., come disproportionately from more privileged backgrounds and as a result this raises the question of access and equity. The National Household Income Consumption and Expenditure Survey (HICES) as cited in Teshome (2006) pointed out that in Ethiopia, not less than 71% tertiary level students come from households in the top income quantile.

However, according to the Council of Higher Education (2001) of South Africa, the world is becoming a knowledge-based society and the role of education, especially at higher level, is the centre of this phenomenon. Given the critical role of universities in socio-economic development, no country can afford not to support at least some higher education institutions of high quality. Such institutions cannot function adequately without reasonable level of state investment. Furthermore, a United Nations Development Programme (UNDP) report as cited in Sawyerr (2004) stated, "it is doubtful that any developing country could make significant progress towards achieving the United Nations Millennium Development Goals for education, universal enrolment in primary education and elimination of gender disparities in primary and secondary education without a strong tertiary education system" (p. 43).

As stated in ESDP III (MoE, 2005), the Ethiopian government allocates about 24-25% of its national budget to education. The share of higher education during the five year planning period was 27.5% of the total education budget. It has become common that many countries (developed/developing) throughout the world practice cost-sharing scheme in their institutions of higher learning. Schwarzenberger & Opheim (2009) stated that the concept of cost sharing in higher education is based on the idea that the costs of higher education should be shared among those who derive public and private benefits from education. Thus, taken into account both private and public benefits of education, it seems reasonable that the individual student (and his/her family) bear a part of the costs of education (p. 157).

Schwarzenberger & Opheim (2009) further indicated that, "although there seems to be a universal acceptance of the cost-sharing rationale, there exist large country differences in the models of cost sharing in higher education, including funding models for higher education and student finance" (p.158). In most African countries, three major forms of cost sharing are being implemented. These are: dual track, up-front and deferred (World Bank, 2010).

Caillaud, F. et al. (2009) indicated that, as of 2009, at least 26 countries in Africa charge some type of tuition fees. Moreover, countries such as Burundi, Cameroon, Cape Verde, the Central African Republic, Chad, the Republic of Congo, Eritrea, Guinea, Mali, Mauritania, Niger, Nigeria (at the federal level) Sudan and Togo do not charge tuition fees or charge insignificant ones.

Various rationales were given by different countries for advocating cost sharing. Some of these include:

- Limited public funds relative to the demand for development and expenditure;
- Tertiary education has high unit costs that cannot easily be borne solely by governments;
- A view that certain members of the society who could afford to pay for the services provided by the public sector should be encouraged to do so;

- Private returns to higher education (higher lifetime earnings, enhanced status etc.) are substantial (and probably extend as well to parents of students);
- Students and families who pay tuition fees will demand accountability and, therefore, universities will have to be more consumer oriented and efficient;
- Allocation and reallocation of the resources will be effected more efficiently where and when cost-sharing takes place;
- Students will be more careful in selecting their field of studies as well as to complete their studies within the given time (Abdena, 2005; Marcucci and Johnstone, 2007).

Johnstone (2004a, 2004b, and 2004c) pointed out that the major rationale for cost sharing is that it promotes equity, efficiency, enhanced student commitment, and improved revenue and institutional services. The equity argument asserts that the beneficiaries in many countries are disproportionately from the upper middle and upper classes that have the ability to pay. The efficiency argument holds that cost sharing encourages institutional efficiency for better teaching, academic programmes and services. The enhanced commitment argument asserts that cost sharing encourages students for faster completion and perhaps can encourage better study. Others argued that as a result of cost-sharing, students will be more prudent in selecting their areas of study, minimize their time in school and become more responsive to changing labour market needs (Obasi & Eboh 2004).

In reference to educational finance, Ethiopia's Education and Training Policy stated that: "the priority for the government financial support will be up to the completion of general education and related training (grade 10) with increased cost-sharing at higher levels of education and training" (p. 31).

In line with this policy statement, the government of Ethiopia introduced a cost-sharing scheme in 2003/04. Even though the aforementioned policy does not articulate the rationale for cost sharing, World Bank (2004) stated, "If the policy works well, it should make the higher education system more accessible, more equitable and more efficient in the allocation of social resources. It should also have positive spill-over effects on the internal managerial efficiency of institutions, which in turn will allow for greater access" (p. 23). The expansion of education and allocation of HEIs budget were not increasing proportionally as the budget lags behind enrolment and this indicates the need to support HEIs budget with cost sharing. The enrolment and budget share of HEIs for the period 2005/06 to 2008/09 is presented in Table 1.

Table 1. Trend of students' enrolment in institutions of higher education in regular program and budget allocation (2003/04-2008/09)

A.Y.	Enrolment	% increase	Education Budget	National budget	% education share of National budget	% of HEIs share of education budget	Budget share of HEIs	% increase
2005/06	93689	-	59906.00	336159.00	17.82	25.3	15156.218	-
2006/07	107960	0.15	76321.00	309982.00	24.62	22.7	19309.213	0.22
2007/08	127033	0.18	93729.00	410709.00	22.82	25.6	23713.437	0.19
2008/09	254192	0.50	113407.00	480352.00	23.61	22.6	28691.971	0.17
% increase from 2005/06 to 2008/09		0.63	-	-	-	-	-	0.47

SOURCE: MOE (2004-2009). Education Statistics Annual Abstracts

Note: The budget share of HEIs is computed using the % of HEIs share of education budget for each year.

The data obtained from the MoE (2005-2009) shows that in 2005/06 the government allocated 17.82% of its total budget for education. In 2008/09, the budget share of education reached 23.61%. Out this total education budget, 22-25% was allocated for higher education. As Table 1 shows student enrolment in 2005/06 was 93,689. In 2008/09, this figure reached 254,192, showing an increase of 63%. However, during the same period, the budget increment was only 47%, indicating the disparity between enrolment and budget allocation. This disparity in higher education budget and enrolment could have been taken as one of the rationale for cost sharing scheme in public HEIs. However, this was not articulated in the proclamations that came out so far.

Since the cost-sharing scheme has been operational for the last eight years, its impact on the quality of the learning-teaching process, resource generation, and improved facilities, quality of student services as well as the problems and challenges have not been studied in detail in public universities. Thus, the purpose of this study was to investigate the implementation of the cost-sharing scheme and its impact on resource generation in public higher education institutions in Ethiopia.

1. 2. General objective of the study

The general objective of this study was to investigate the impact of the cost-sharing scheme in enhancing revenue generation in order to improve the teaching/learning environment. Moreover, the study attempted to assess the problems/challenges experienced by students as well as government bodies, such as the Ethiopian Revenues and Customs Authority (ERCA) on issues related to cost sharing.

The specific objectives of the study were to:

1. investigate the implementation of cost sharing scheme in selected government higher education institutions, taking Addis Ababa and Adama Universities as the focus of the study,
2. assess the observed impact of cost sharing scheme in enhancing resource generation by soliciting the opinions of students, university management (especially heads of cost sharing units) as well as staff members concerning issues related to cost-sharing scheme,
3. assess the challenges/problems encountered by government bodies, such as the Ethiopian Revenues and Customs Authority in collecting student loans,
4. highlight the best practices of other countries (mainly African countries) in implementing cost sharing scheme.

In order to address the objectives stated above, the following major research questions were formulated.

1.3. Basic research questions

1. What mechanisms were used to determine the amount of cost sharing in Ethiopian higher education institutions?
2. How far did the stakeholders participate in determining the amount of cost sharing?
3. To what extent is the cost-sharing scheme implemented in selected government higher education institutions?
4. What is the perception of students and instructors on the impact of cost sharing on the quality of learning-teaching, availability of resources and facilities, budget, and student services in public universities?
5. What major problems/challenges were encountered in Ethiopian HEIs in implementing the cost sharing scheme?
6. How effective is the system designed by the government to collect cost sharing payments?

1.4. Significance of the study

The outcome this study could benefit policy makers and implementers, university management bodies, staff members, researchers, students, as well as other stakeholders to understand the implementation of cost sharing in Ethiopian higher education institutions. Furthermore, it could help to understand and overcome the challenges facing the cost sharing scheme in the Ethiopian context.

1.5. Delimitations

Currently, there are twenty-two government institutions of higher learning and a significant number of private colleges and universities enrolling thousands of students. This study included only two government institutions of higher learning, namely Adama and Addis Ababa Universities.

1.6. Limitations of the Study

The introduction of cost sharing in Ethiopia is a recent phenomenon, which limits the availability of data on its implementation. The organizations to implement cost sharing included: MoE, HEIs, Ministry of Health, Ethiopian Revenues and Customs Authority, and Employers. To get full data from these organizations proved difficult. However, effort was made to get hold of available data. Furthermore, since this study focused on Addis Ababa and Adama universities, the findings could not be fully generalized to all institutions of higher learning.

2. Review of Related Literature

2. 1. The concept of Cost sharing

Cost-sharing in higher education has been defined as a shift in the burden of higher education costs from being borne exclusively or predominantly by government or taxpayers to being shared with parents and students (Johnstone 2004a, 2004b, and 2004c; Ishengoma, 2004; Marcucci & Johnstone 2007, Marcucci, Johnstone & Ngolovi, 2008; Johnstone & Marcucci, 2010; World Bank, 2010). It consists of tuition fee, cost of food, lodging and others.

The word tuition, in the United States refers a fee for instruction. In the United Kingdom and most of the rest of the world, however, the word tuition means instruction, so fee for instruction is called tuition fee (Johnstone and Marcucci, 2010).

The term tuition designates a fee paid to cover part of the cost of instruction. It properly refers to mandatory charges levied upon all students paid by themselves or their families covering some portion of the general underlying cost of instruction. Fees on the other hand can consist of several types of charges. Fees are generally referred to as charges levied to cover almost all expenses associated with particular institutionally provided goods or services that are frequently (although not always) partaken by some (but not all) students and that neglect in other circumstances, be privately provided. Such fees, for example, might cover some or all of the costs of food and lodging or health and transportation services or some other special expenses associated with instruction, such as consumable supplies in an art class or transportation associated with special internship experience (Johnstone & Marcucci, 2010). There are other charges, such as application, registration, examination, remarking fees and other similar costs, which are considered fees.

Teshome (2007) defined cost sharing in Ethiopia as "a scheme by which beneficiaries of public higher education institutions and the government share the cost incurred for the purposes of education and other services. A beneficiary is any student at a public institution pursuing higher education/training and who has entered into an obligation for the future payment of the cost of his/her education/training and other services, as the case may be" (p.177).

Cost-sharing in higher education can be viewed as being borne by four principal parties: (1) the government or taxpayers; (2) parents; (3) students; and/or (4) individual or institutional donor (Johnstone, 2004a). In the Ethiopian situation, 85% of the tuition fee is borne by the government and 15% by the students in addition to the full coverage of the food, dormitory fees and health fees. It also provides provision for parents to cover the cost of their children.

In Ethiopian higher education, beneficiaries of public higher education and those who enter an agreement (that is, students) are required to share full costs related to food and lodging and a minimum of 15 per cent of the tuition cost. The cost of food is basically the cost of the foodstuff only – not including any cost of personnel, administration and other costs (Teshome, 2007).

Students pay their cost sharing through a graduate tax. Graduate tax involves the application of a flat graduate tax collected as a percentage of salary over a lifetime or a set period of years - 15 years in the Ethiopian case. A graduate tax scheme was introduced in the 2003/04 academic year, which is a version of an income related system of deferred payments. The Ethiopian graduate tax has the following repayment characteristics (Chapman 2005, p.40):

- payments to be collected from beneficiaries on the basis of a formula calculated as a percentage (proposed as 10 per cent) of annual income, automatically deducted from salaries;
- the exemption of around 35 per cent of students from payment of the tax, those who would be teachers and other professionals deemed to be of public interest; and
- a discount of 5% for an up-front payment and for those who can pay on an on-going basis up to the end of the grace period, which is one year after graduation.

The World Bank has broadly applauded the Ethiopian graduate tax scheme, but offers some telling criticisms, including that:

- the minimum repayment rate of 10 per cent looks to be very high for Ethiopian graduates given their levels of income;
- excusing a large number of graduates from any repayment obligations is questionable, and if they were also subjected to payments the high rate of 10 per cent could be reduced;
- the 5 per cent discount for up-front payments seem to be too low to encourage upfront payments (Chapman, 2005, p. 40).

Ethiopia has responded to the 5 percent discount for upfront payment with the issuance of Higher Education Cost-Sharing Council of Ministers Regulation No. 154/2008 that vests the authority to set discount for upfront payment of tuition fee to the MoE. In its guidelines of 2009, MoE has set the following discounts for those beneficiaries who would pay upfront their cost sharing at different times. (a) a discount of 10% for upfront payments at the time of registration; (b) a discount of 5% for upfront payments every year during their university education and (c) a discount of 3% for upfront payments during the grace period (MoE, 2009).

Compared to the discount for upfront payment in other countries, these discounts are still low to motivate the parents of the students to make up front payments. For instance, the Australian Education Contribution Scheme provides 20% discount for upfront payment of tuition fees (Johnstone, 2004c, Johnstone & Marcucci, 2010).

2.2. Rationale for cost sharing

The main conventional rationales for cost sharing and revenue diversification in higher education worldwide are: (a) greater equity (the notion that those who benefit should at least share in the costs), both through a better alignment of those who bear the costs and those who reap the benefits as well as through the expanded participation of those who had formerly been left out; (b) improved efficiency (the notion that the payment of some tuition will make students and families more discerning consumers, and the universities more cost-conscious providers); (c) responsiveness (the idea that the need to supplement public revenue with tuition will make universities more responsive to individual and societal needs) (d) sheer need for revenue sources what may be the most important - and certainly less controversial- rationale is that the government needs revenue for expansion, quality, access, and participation (Johnstone 20004a, and World Bank, 2010).

Johnstone as cited in Schwarzenberger, and Opheim (2009) indicated that the rationale of cost-sharing in higher education is based on the idea that the costs of higher education should be shared among those who benefit from education. This notion includes the idea that higher education is as an investment, which involves costs and benefits for both the society and for the individual. Thus, taken into account both private and public benefits of education, it seems reasonable that the individual student (and his/her family) bears at least a part of the costs of education (Schwarzenberger & Opheim 2009, p.157). In most countries of the world, the need for cost sharing is rationalized as a result of increasing public and private demand for higher education, as well as increasing per-student costs in higher education (Johnstone, 2004a).

Marcucci & Johnstone (2007) stated the rationale for cost sharing as governments increasingly turning to cost sharing in order to meet the growing demand for, and decreasing government investment in, public higher education. They further stated that tuition fees are critical both for the very considerable revenue at stake and for the potential impact on higher education accessibility and the implications for equity and social justice.

Salerno (2006) noted that cost sharing has received greater endorsement in the developing world and particularly in sub-Saharan Africa than anywhere else. A shortage of public funding, rapidly expanding enrollments, and strong endorsement from international aid agencies like the World Bank have all worked in concert to push cost sharing as the way for such nations to strengthen their fragile higher education sectors and spur economic growth.

In the Ethiopian context, the rationale for cost sharing is prioritization of education and reduction of unit cost per student. The education funding priority of the Ethiopian government is primary (grades 1-8) and general secondary (grades 9 and 10) education. In this regard the Ethiopian Education and Training Policy (ETP) (1994) states that "The priority for government financial support will be up to the completion of general secondary education and related training (grade 10) with increased cost sharing at higher levels of education and Training" (p. 31).

The Education Sector Development Program III (ESDP III) (MoE, 2005) also suggested cost sharing as effective measure to reduce unit cost of education and has planned to raise the cost shared by higher education institution students from 2005/6 to 2009/10 from 31.11 to 123.30 million Birr (MOE, 2005).

Cost sharing was introduced in order to increase the enrolment of students in higher education and expand higher education significantly beyond the existing level. This decision led to the increase in enrolment in government higher education institutions in under graduate programs from 36,049 in 2002/03 to 107, 980 in 2006/07 (MoE, 2008). Such huge expansion requires revenue that can be generated through the implementation of cost sharing in HEIs.

A study by Lee (1992) showed that the rationale of equity remains an elusive goal as cost sharing has not succeeded in equalizing educational opportunity. The study found that a young person's chance of continuing education after high school depends on ability to pay the price of attendance and on academic achievement. In Ethiopia, student achievement plays a decisive role as admission to HEIs is determined by academic achievement of students at the tenth grade national examinations. Students who enrolled in the preparatory secondary education are placed in HEIs with the use of University Entrance Examination (UEE) (MoE 2009).

2.3. Tuition Fees Setting Policies in HEIs

According to Johnstone & Marcucci (2010), tuition fees are set under the following circumstances.

(1) The cultural and historical acceptance of public sector fees generally;

(2) The existence of other kinds of nondiscretionary supposedly non-tuition fees in addition to what is acknowledged to be official tuition fee;

(3) The underlying per student costs of instruction that are taken as the basis of tuition fee;

(4) The mix of private as opposed to public benefits perceived to be attached to the institution or academic program (which is almost the same as identifying the market value attached to an institution or program;

(5) The prevailing cost of student living (net of institutional or government subsidies for food, lodging and other expenses); and

(6) The amount and coverage of student financial assistance.

The basis of tuition fee for most of the countries in the world including Ethiopia is the underlying per student cost of instruction. This cost of instruction varies by country, institution, system or program.

The authority of setting tuition fees at public higher education institutions is vested in different entities in different countries. The tuition policy of a country is generally dependent on a law or other type of legal instrument that provides the basis for charging or for prohibiting tuition fees. The USA, Canada, Japan, India, South Korea, the Philippines and some of the Anglophone nations in Africa have national and/or state policies requiring moderate tuition fees in most or all public higher educational institutions. In China, the 1998 Higher Education Law calls for the charging of tuition fees to all students (Marcucci &Johnstone, 2010).

Other countries have laws that prohibit the charging of tuition fees. In Central and Eastern Europe, Russia and the other countries of the former Soviet Union, free higher education is frequently guaranteed by their constitutions or framework laws (Johnstone 204a, Johnstone 2004b, Johnstone, 2007). In Nigeria the government announced in May 2002 that the 24 federal universities were forbidden to charge tuition or other academic fees (Obasi & Eboh, 2002). In Ireland, government efforts to reinstate tuition fees, abolished in 1996, met with failure in the summer of 2003 (Marcucci & Johnstone, 2007).

In Germany, the federal framework law imposed restrictions on the authority of individual state to charge tuition fees, and the Social Democratic Government banned tuition fees for the first degree outright (Ziegele as cited in Marcucci & Johnstone, 2007). Certain exceptions were made, and several states implemented the special forms of fees that were allowed, such as tuition fees for students who exceeded the normal duration of a certain programme, plus four semesters and tuition fees for students enrolled in a second degree. In January of 2005, the country's Supreme Court overturned the ban in a case brought by six states and ruled that individual states could introduce tuition fees. As of 2005, several states plan to pass enabling legislation and impose fees of about 500 Euros, while others have no intention of changing their tuition policies (World Bank, 2010).

The World Bank (2010) noted that in many countries, including Canada, India and the USA, tuition fees are set at the state or provincial level. In Hong Kong and the UK the central government is responsible for setting tuition fee levels. And in others, such as Chile and South Korea, the individual institutions are authorized to set their own tuition fees.

In Australia, universities have the power to increase their tuitions by up to 25% above current levels (Wright, 2008). In several countries, tuition fee setting authority is split between the central and state governments or between the state and institutions. In The Netherlands, for example, the government sets tuition fees for those students eligible for student support and the institutions set tuition fees for the students who are not eligible (i.e. part-time students, students who have used up all of their entitlement for student support and students whose personal income exceeds the income limits for student support) (Marcucci & Johnstone, 2007).

In Japan, a major reform in 2004 authorized the national universities to incorporate as public corporations and to set their own tuition fees. However, universities may not exceed 110% of the standard fee set by the Ministry of Education and the Ministry of Finance. The local authorities continue to determine the tuition fee levels at local public institutions (Marcucci & Johnstone, 2007). In Nigeria, the federal government has forbidden the charging of tuition fees at the federal universities, but universities that are owned and financed by the states are allowed to set their own tuition fees (Marcucci & Johnstone, 2007).

In Ethiopia, the Education and Training Policy (ETP, 1994), Proclamation No. 154/2008 (FDRE, 2008) and the Higher Education Proclamation (FDRE, 2009) provided the framework for cost sharing in higher educational institutions. The Higher Education Cost-Sharing Regulation issued by the Council of Ministers (Regulation No. 154/2008, FDRE, 2008) states that beneficiaries of HEIs share 15% if the instructional fees which each respective institution determines. The Higher Education Proclamation No. 650/2009 (FDRE, 2009) stipulates that a public institution may charge tuition fees, which shall be determined by the board and may constitute payments in cash or in service (Articles 91 and 92). In exceptional cases, medicine graduates who discontinue to cover their cost sharing in terms of services, are obliged to pay full costs of their education plus 50% penalty.

2.4. Types of Cost Sharing Policies in HEIs

Worldwide three types of tuition fees are implemented in cost sharing (Marcucci & Johnstone, 2007). These are: up front, dual track and deferred tuition fees. Up front tuition fee is based on the premises of an officially expected parental contribution and the assumption is that they are able to provide it (Johnstone & Marcucci, 2010). Deferred tuition fees on the other hand are based on the premises that a student is financially dependent adult responsible for his or her expenses including the share of instructional costs that is presented by the tuition fee.

Dual track refers to the two tracks of students with respect to tuition fees where one track of students are charged no or very nominal tuition fee and the other track are charged substantial tuition fee for the pursuit of the same degree program at the same institution. Dual track tuition fee is common in Russia, Eastern Europe, and East Africa. In East Africa the dual track tuition fee was first implemented in Uganda (Makarere University) in 1992 followed by the University of Nairobi in 1998 and then by most of universities in the region (Court, 1999;Kiamba, 2003). North and West Africa and the Middle East are politically unable to accept tuition fees other than very nominal tuition fees (Johnstone & Marcucci, 2010). Table 2 presents some examples of worldwide types of tuition fees in public universities (World Bank, 2010).

Table 2. Worldwide Types of Public Tuition Fee Policies

Up-front	No tuition		Dual-track	Deferred
Austria	The Netherlands	Brazil	Australia	Australia Scotland
Belgium	Nigeria (State)	Denmark	Egypt	New Zealand
Canada	Norway	Finland	Ethiopia	Ethiopia
Chile	Philippines	France	Hungary	England (as of 2006)
China	Portugal	Francophone Africa	Kenya	Wales (as of 2007)
England (now)	Singapore		Poland	
Hong Kong	South Africa	Germany	Romania	
India	Spain	Greece	Russia	
Italy	Turkey	Ireland	Tanzania	
	United States	Luxembourg	Uganda	

Japan	Wales (now)	Malta	Vietnam
Kenya		Nigeria (Federal)	
Korea		Sweden	
Mexico			
Mongolia			

SOURCE: World Bank (2010)

According to Caillaud et. al., 2009, World Bank (2010), as of 2009 at least 26 countries in Africa charge some type of tuition fee. The three major types of tuition fee policies: up front, dual track and deferred exist in Africa. In some countries the tuition fee polices combine these major types of tuition fee polices shown in Table 2.

Up front tuition fee in Africa. Up front tuition fee requires students (or parents or extended families) to pay a tuition fee for a semester or academic year at the beginning of that semester or year. Sometimes the proportion of tuition fee to be paid or the amount of financial assistance available depends on a family's income. The number of African countries where up-front tuition fees have been introduced is growing, even in some Francophone countries such as Cote d'Ivoire and the Democratic Republic of Congo, where free higher education has long been considered an untouchable right (World Bank, 2010).

Dual track tuition fee in Africa. The second type of tuition fee is dual track which is based on the need of the government or the institution to ration a limited number places that are free (or nearly free) for political or legal reasons, generally using a single examination, while allowing another tuition fee paying track or tracks for the desperately needed revenue supplementation (Marcucci, Johnstone & Ngolovi, 2008).

In Africa, two distinct types of dual-track tuition fee policies are being implemented. The first type used in countries such as Ghana, Uganda, Tanzania, and Kenya, awards free or low-cost places to a limited number of students based on their performance on the secondary school–leaving exam and fee-paying places to others who score lower but still meet entrance criteria or, as in Angola and Ethiopia, to those who study in the evening or during the summer. The second type, used in countries such as Benin, Madagascar, and Senegal that offer free places to all students passing the high school–leaving baccalaureate exam in faculties with open access and fee-paying places in the more competitive professional faculties or institutions.

The dual track policy was introduced in Uganda at Makerere University via the Private Entry Scheme (PES) in 1992 and later extended to all Uganda public universities. Under the dual track tuition fee paying students go two stage admission processes: Public Universities Joint Admissions Board (PUJAB) and PES (Court, 1999). First, all students are required to fill in PUJAB application forms for government sponsored places where top students are provided scholarship on the basis of Uganda Advanced Certificate of Education Examination (UACE).

The second admissions process for private admission happens after the PUJAB admissions. Students who do not get a government scholarship are invited to put their applications under the PES arrangement. There are a few students who get government scholarships for a program that was not their first choice, but who reapply under PES. The private admission selection process is similar to the PUJAB process, and public universities do the admissions jointly (Marcucci, Johnstone & Ngolovi, 2008).

In Kenya, students join higher education institutions through Modules I and II programs similar to that of Uganda. In Module I program, the government covers most of the costs of education leaving the remaining cost to the students to raise from the Kenyan Higher Education Loan Board (HELB) which carries 4 percent interest rate. Students who attain the prescribed cut off point (COP) are admitted into Module I state supported programs through the Joints Admissions Board (JAB). For instance, in 2004 the average cost for each degree program was US $ 1, 534 per year of which the government covered US $895 leaving the remaining US$639 to the student to raise from HELB or private sources (Marcucci, Johnstone & Ngolovi, 2008). In Module II program students who meet the minimum requirements for admission to universities on self-paying basis. Both self-sponsored and government sponsored students attend classes together.

Since students enrolled in Module I program are required to wait one year after they have completed high school or if were placed in academic programs that they have no desire to pursue, some students turn down their places in the module I programs and enrol into the self–paying program. Enrolling in the module II programs, therefore, offers students a chance to complete their education sooner than those individuals enrolled in the module I program and also enables them to pursue the courses they desire (Kiamba, 2004 & Otieno, 2004).

In Tanzania, a dual track tuition policy was introduced in a context in which cost sharing was already underway in higher education (Marcucci, Johnstone & Ngolovi, 2008). In 1992, students and families became responsible for paying for their own transportation; application, registration, entry exam and student union fees as well as allowances were eliminated (Marcucci, Johnstone &

Ngolovi, 2008). In 1996, the University of Dar es Salaam's Council approved an official proposal for admitting privately sponsored Tanzanian students in 2002. It officially recommended that the university fill remaining spots not filled with government sponsored students (who did not have to pay tuition fees) with privately sponsored, tuition fee paying students. In the same year, it voted to give the sons, daughters and spouses of university staff and members of the University Council the right to pay only half of the tuition fees (Ishengoma, 2004).

The dual track tuition policy in Tanzania was discontinued when the government introduced student loans in July 2005 for the 2005-06 academic year to cover tuition fees, other academic fees, room and board for all higher education students whether government or privately sponsored in the public universities or self paying in the private universities. This student loan policy dramatically changed the country's tuition policy, moving it from a dual track policy to one in which all students must pay tuition, albeit deferred as a loan to be repaid once they have finished their studies (Marcucci, Johnstone & Ngolovi, 2008).

Deferred tuition fee in Africa. In a deferred tuition policy, the tuition fee is expected from the student rather than from the family, which is deferred as a loan. Such a policy has the political advantage of somewhat disguising the implementation of a tuition fee, although it essentially forgoes some or perhaps most of the revenue that might be forthcoming from a family contribution that is attached to an "up-front" tuition fee.

Because student loan schemes are generally used to cover student-borne costs of living, including food, housing, and other essentials, there has been a juxtaposition between (a) tuition fees that are deferred (generally paid by the student) as opposed to up front generally paid by families; and (b) income-contingent as opposed to fixed-schedule repayment obligations for students loans. This has led to considerable policy confusion. Income-contingent loans are generally thought to work best when they can be collected by employers at the point of wage or salary payments along with deductions for income tax withholding and pension obligations as is the case in Australia or the United Kingdom. The scheme works much less well in Sub-Saharan African countries, where tax identification numbers are not yet ubiquitous and where university graduates are much more likely to hold multiple jobs, be self-employed, or work outside the country (Johnstone, 2006). Deferred fees- wherein the students, regardless of parental wealth, are considered ultimately responsible for a share of higher education costs - exist in Africa, in only Botswana, Ethiopia, and Lesotho. In these three countries, all students who have been admitted to university may defer their tuition fees and repay them as a student loan following graduation or departure from the university (World Bank, 2010).

The policies in Namibia (adopted in 1997), Rwanda (adopted in 2003, with means testing beginning in 2008), and Tanzania (adopted in 2005) conform more to a model of "up-front" tuition in which parents are responsible for the higher education costs of their children with a deferred fee option only available for needy students. Eligibility for the deferred fees with income-contingent repayment options are means tested based on parental income and those students who are not eligible for the loan or who are eligible for only part of the loan have to pay their tuition fees up-front (World Bank, 2010).

In Ghana, Atuahene (2009) noted that as part of the solution to the financial challenges faced by the universities a student loans scheme was introduced in 1971-72. However, the scheme faced problems in the recovery of loans. Within the eleven years of its operation, students owed a total of US$ 375,560 to the scheme but only US$2, 074 was paid back. In 1989 the policy was modified and the Social Security and National Insurance Trust (SSNIT), an organization in charge of pension and retirement programmes in Ghana was added to participate in the scheme. One important aspect of the new policy was that government heavily subsidized the interest rate. Students were supposed to pay 3 percent, which was increased, to 6 percent in the 1990s. With these favourable repayment terms, alleged administrative inefficiencies by the SSNIT, and poor loan recovery mechanism and because graduates do not secure jobs immediately after graduation, the operation of a scheme suffered a deficit of US$16 million due to high default rates on the part of the government and students.

A graduate tax is a variant on the income-contingent loan, in which the student, in return for low or no tuition fees, becomes obligated after graduation to pay an income surtax generally for the rest of his or her earning lifetime with no "balances owed" and no way to prepay or exit the obligation (Johnstone, 2006). While no country has a formal graduate tax at the present time, the income-contingent repayment obligation in Ethiopia is actually called a "graduate tax."

According to Teshome (2007), the Ethiopian government adopted cost sharing in the form of Graduate Tax Scheme in 2003. Graduate Tax Scheme is the modified form of the Australian Income Contingent Repayment System where the payment of the cost is to be effected in a form of a tax payable from the salary or other earnings obtained after graduation. Graduate tax is a scheme to supplement revenue but not to replace government investment in higher education (Teshome, 2007, p. 180). Table 3 presents the type of tuition fee policies being implemented in selected African Countries. The Ethiopian graduate tax scheme is a deferred tax fee with upfront payments for those who can afford.

Table 3. Types of tuition fee policies in Africa

Up-front	Dual track	Deferred and dual track	Up front and deferred	No tuition
Cote de Ivore	Angola	Kenya	Namibia	Gabón
Gambia	Benin	Rwanda	Ethiopia	Burundi
Liberia	Botswana	Tanzania	Lesotho	Cameroon
Mozambique	Burkina Faso		Swaziland	Cape Verde
Nigeria (State level)	Egypt			Central Africa Republic
	Ghana			Chad
Sierra Leone	Madagascar			The Republic of Congo
South Africa	Malawi			Guinea
	Mauritius			Mali
	Uganda			Mauritania
	Zambia			Níger
	Zimbabwe			Nigeria (Federal)
				Sudan
				Togo
				Francophone Africa

SOURCE: World Bank (2010)

2.5. The financial significance of tuition fees

The significance of tuition fee is reflected in the amount of revenue collected from cost sharing and its effect in increasing enrolment (Table 4).

In Uganda from 1997-2006 student enrolment increased from 14,400 to 34,500. During the same period, university financing changed profoundly and the share of private financing in the university budget grew from 30 to 60 percent. Public financing per student was maintained for government-sponsored students only whose number only increased from 6,710 to 6,948. However, these students represented a declining portion of the total number of students falling from 46 to 20 percent, while the average public resources per student decreased by 50 percent. Nevertheless, this situation has improved since 2001. In sum, public and private resources per student have decreased 10 percent since 1997.

Certainly, the dual track tuition policy has had an extraordinarily beneficial effect on the financial viability of Makerere and Nairobi, and it is presumed also to have had a somewhat positive impact on the University of Dar es Salaam, Kenyatta University, and other higher educational institutions where it has been introduced (Marcucci, Johnstone & Ngolovi, 2008).

Table 4. The Financial Significance of Tuition Fees in African Countries

Insignificant (≤ 10%)	Significant (11–29%)	Very significant (>30%)
Tanzania	Namibia	Benin (selective programs)
Zimbabue	South Africa	Kenya (module II)
Madagascar	Swaziland	Mauritius (University of Technology,
Malawi (residencial)	Ethiopia	Mauritius)
Mozambique	Kenya (module I)	Uganda (fee paying)
Rwanda (government supported)	Rwanda (privately paying science courses)	Zambia (fee paying)
		Burkina Faso (elite institutions)
		Ghana
		Kenya
		Malawi (nonresidential)
		Rwanda (privately paying non science courses)
		Nigeria (state universities)

SOURCE: World Bank (2010)

Atuahene (2009) reported that the Ghana Education Trust Fund (GETF) was introduced in 2000. In this scheme, the Internal Revenue Service was required to increase the already existing Value Added Tax rate from 10 percent to 12.5 percent of which 2.5 percent was scheduled for the GETF account to supplement government budgetary allocation to higher education. The GETF was the second major source of finance to the education sector contributing 10 percent and 12.9 percent to government expenditure in 2006 and 2008 respectively. It contributed to massive enrolment increase from 63,576 in 2003/04 to 88, 445 in 2006/07 and financed over 500 different projects most of which were the construction and rehabilitation of buildings. The GETF is making significant contributions toward higher education development in Ghana in the areas of infrastructure, student development and support, faculty research and development, support for mathematics, science and technical education and robust support to the Ministry of Education and its agencies.

The GETF has a potential for the replication and adaptation by developing countries facing similar problems in financing higher education in Africa. According to Teshome (2007) the contribution of the Ethiopian graduate tax may improve access and quality of HEIs through government investment, although the cost shared is not direct revenue or is not directly recovered by the institutions themselves. (p. 181). The government invests in higher education as an important sector in anticipation of some cost recovery in the future. This will help the expansion of access and improvement of quality of higher education.

Marcucci & Johnstone (2009, p.38) concluded that "little is known empirically worldwide about the impact of cost sharing and tuition fees on higher education accessibility and enrolment behaviour, or about the ameliorative efficiency of programmes, such as means-tested grants and loans. They have suggested additional research is needed in order to inform higher education policymaking". Similarly, the guidelines of MoE (2009) stated that "the institution shall inform the beneficiaries that the cost shared is a very small amount from the total cost of the institution and the payment shall be collected after five and six years. This means that the small amount of payment the student shares cannot bring any change on the quality of education."(p. 5).

2.6. Cost Sharing Recovery in HEIs

Cost recovery from graduate tax schemes depends on the ability of the government to collect the entire loan repayment with interest as part of an existing and ubiquitous system of tax withholding and/or pension contribution imposed on employers (University of Dar es Salaam, 2002).

Higher education institutions in Africa generate on average about 30 percent of their income; and this ranges from less than 5 percent in Madagascar and Zimbabwe to 56 percent in Uganda and 75 percent in Guinea-Bissau (World Bank 2010). Uganda is implementing dual-track tuition policies whereby a certain number of free or very low-cost university places are awarded based on criteria such as academic excellence, income level, or positive discrimination, while other places are available on a tuition fee–paying basis or deferred-tuition policy. Even in some Francophone countries, such as Benin, where free higher education had long been considered a right, some public universities have chosen to charge fees for professional programs or programs of excellence (World Bank, 2010).

Johnstone (2004c) suggested effective cost recovery can be accomplished through a diminution of the subsidies on student loans (similar to the diminution in the value of non-repayable grants), an increase in interest rates, or a reduction in the length of time that interest is not charged, or through a reduction in the numbers of loans for which the repayments for any number of reasons are forgiven. Or the effective cost recovery might be accomplished through a tightening of collections or a reduction in the instances of default with no change in the effective rates of interest paid by those who were repaying anyway.

Cost recovery remains the main challenge in most countries for student loans to be effective and sustainable. The main issues facing student loans stem from interest rates that are set far too low, grace periods and repayment periods that are unnecessarily long and exacerbate the losses, and loans that are implemented in such a way that students are frequently unaware that they are incurring a real repayment obligation. In addition, legal systems often make debt collection expensive (World Bank, 2010). In Ethiopia (FDRE, 2003 and 2008) the powers and duties for implementation of cost sharing in HEIs are shared by the MoE, the Ethiopian Revenue and Customs Authority, HEIs and employers, which complicates the recovery of cost sharing. Another factor that complicates the recovery of cost sharing is poor record keeping which cannot adequately keep track of students or graduates (University of Dar es Salaam, 2002). This is particularly true in Ethiopia where the record cannot provide complete information about the current status of beneficiaries and makes tracing them very difficult.

A graduate tax scheme will almost certainly not provide significant cost recovery in most transitional and developing countries for the simple reason that most do not have effective and reliable systems of collection. In the absence of such ubiquitous systems, governments are likely to know the incomes of and be able to collect from mainly the civil servants and perhaps those employed by multinational corporations and some large private enterprises. However, repayments are likely to be low or missing altogether from those employed in first or second jobs in the private sector, many or most of those who are self-employed, and virtually all émigrés-----a significant proportion of the university graduates of many transitional and developing countries (University of Dar es Salaam, 2002). Furthermore, insufficient numbers of jobs in African economies challenge the ability of university graduates to repay their loans (World Bank, 2010, p. 26).

In Ethiopia, cost sharing is to be recovered from students in the form of graduate tax after their graduation. The beneficiary, the employing organization and the Ethiopian Revenues and Customs Authority legally have duties to make effective the cost sharing recovery program (FDRE, 2008). The repayment or recovery of cost is effected on the basis of the legally binding agreement that a beneficiary entered into with the institutions at the beginning of each academic year. With this contract, the beneficiary has given his/her agreement that the amount owed will be paid from future earnings in the form of tax deductions according to the provisions laid down by law (Teshome, 2007).

As cited in Teshome (2007), Johnstone and Abebayehu stressed that the Ethiopian graduate tax will not provide significant alternative non-governmental revenue. They suggested a modest upfront tuition fee in addition to a gradual lowering of subsidies for room and board. These were supported by Teshome (2007) who stated that "the revenue collected by the graduate tax scheme may not be significant, particularly in the light of the huge amount of budget and investment required to expand access and maintain quality and ensure relevance" (p.187). It was estimated that the recovery rate could be as high as 10% during the initial years and 20% after the year 2015 with a default rate of 30% (Teshome, 2007).

Teshome (2007, p. 184) identified graduate tax in the Ethiopian context as having certain drawbacks: (a) inability to recover money for several years. Recovery from taxation only begins after four to five years after the introduction of the scheme. It is likely to be a decade or more before the system begins properly to pay for itself or reach a break-even point. Even then, the repayments are unlikely to be sufficient to cover the new loans in the light of discounted present value and likely default rates; (b) absence of guarantee that the universities would receive the additional funding raised except for the relatively small amount of upfront payments; (c) presence of possibilities that beneficiaries may avoid repayment making the scheme unattractive and an ineffective alternative revenue source. Information about the beneficiaries' whereabouts is not centrally or regionally well documented; (d) requirement of efficient and modern taxation mechanisms to keep track of the increasing number graduates where such system is not present in Ethiopia; and (e) failure of beneficiaries to acknowledge their full income for the purpose of the graduate tax repayment will be difficult due to the general nature of most people in avoiding taxable income declarations. These drawbacks may result in making the scheme of cost sharing in higher education ineffective. For cost recovery to be effective, tightening of the collection system is mandatory, which is so far not well established from the observations of these writers.

Some defaults are expected under the graduate tax system implemented in Ethiopia. Some of the reasons for the defaults could be (Teshome, 2007): (a) lack of information about the whereabouts of the beneficiary after graduation; (b) the less controlled mobility of beneficiaries outside of the country; and (c) weakness in the tax collection mechanisms. Effective recovery of education cost is observed by medicine graduates who could only get their academic credentials for studying abroad and employment after paying educational fees. A medicine graduate pays up to Birr 500,000.00 which include total education fee plus 50% penalty to get his/her diploma if he/she discontinued serving in the assigned government health institution.

The generally high rates of default on student loans are the main danger for student loan schemes in any country and are especially pernicious in Sub-Saharan Africa due to several factors, including (a) the absence in most countries of a widespread credit culture that understands the meaning of credit and the obligations that follow, especially outside the middle class in the metropolitan centres; (b) the weakness of the economies and the high rates of unemployment even after college or university graduation; (c) the prevalence of emigration, which further complicates collection; and (d) a resentment of (and resistance to) the entire notion of cost sharing, especially in the Francophone countries but extending to all of Sub- Saharan Africa (World Bank 2010).

The following ten major patterns explain the failure in recovering payment and ensuring the financial sustainability of student loans (World Bank. 2010, pp. 90-94).

One, inadequate means testing allows students to borrow who have no real financial need. Most of the loan programs in Africa are not predicated on the financial soundness of a student and his or her family but is made available in some cases to all students and is targeted in others to students who are needy, from certain underprivileged regions or in certain academic fields. Nine of the 13 loan programs in Africa use means testing in the awarding of loans, while in Ethiopia, Lesotho, and Swaziland, loans are available to all higher education students. Means testing has been criticized for not targeting truly needy students. Some countries, such as Tanzania, have improved their data collection to have a more accurate assessment of the socio-economic situation of applicants and their families.

Two, interest rates are set far too low generally by politicians fearful of student resistance to cost sharing, which is often associated with student loans. Four of the loan programs charge no interest (Botswana, Lesotho, Malawi, and Tanzania, although the Higher Education Students Loans Board [HESLB] in Tanzania is working to change this. Of the other nine that do charge interest, only three countries, namely Ghana, South Africa, and Ethiopia, charge a real interest rate, i.e. greater than the prevailing rate of inflation, and only four, viz. Ghana, Kenya, Rwanda, and South Africa, compound interest during the in-school years and grace period. This means that in more than half of the programs, significant interest subsidies are built into the program, which has a negative impact on cost recovery.

Three, grace periods and repayment periods are unnecessarily long and exacerbate the losses from the excessive subsidization of interest. Repayment periods in African student loan programs range from very short, as in Lesotho and Namibia, to indefinite, as in South Africa.

Four, loans are disbursed in such a way that students are frequently unaware that they are incurring a real repayment obligation. Loans in Africa are mainly disbursed directly to the higher education institute to cover tuition fees and to the student to cover living costs. However, in countries with fully deferred tuition fees, such as Botswana, Ethiopia, and Lesotho, students never see any of the money, which may limit their understanding of their repayment obligations.

Five, many of the student loan programs in Africa forgive all or part of the loan under certain conditions. A loan may be forgiven if a student successfully completes his or her program, studies in a certain field, or lives or works in a certain location after graduation. In Ethiopia, teachers and other professionals deemed to be of public interest are exempted from paying the so-called graduate tax. In Lesotho, those who work in the public sector are required to pay back only 50 percent of the loan, those who work in the private sector are required to pay back 65 percent of the loan, and those who work outside Lesotho are required to repay 100 percent of the loan. In Botswana, students who studied on programs for which there is a shortage of personnel in the country receive forgiveness of all the tuition fees and maintenance costs they owe.

Six, legal systems make debt collection expensive and frequently unsuccessful. Regarding legal enforcement, some student loan programs in Africa, including Kenya, Ghana, Tanzania, and Rwanda, were established with weak or nonexistent enabling legislation, and it was only when semiautonomous boards were established with real enforcement powers for collecting loans or for requiring employers to collect loans that real cost recovery began.

Seven, the adequacy of student loans to cover all costs is an important factor in their recovery. If loans are not large enough to cover all costs, this may discourage students from low socio-economic backgrounds from attending their college education at all. Inadequate loans may also lead students to live in substandard conditions or not get enough to eat and ultimately to drop out and have a difficult time finding employment. It is significantly more difficult to collect from unemployed borrowers. In Burkina Faso, for example, students complain that the maximum loan is inadequate to meet university fees and living expenses. Similarly, in Kenya, loan amounts may be adequate for government-sponsored students, but they are not adequate to cover all costs for self-financed students.

Eight, underdeveloped administrative systems and inadequate staffing do not allow the system to recover significant repayment. In many of the loan programs in Africa, overworked government bureaucracies are expected to run the student loan schemes in addition to their other work, and they face inadequate staffing, resources, and consultation procedures with other stakeholders. Loan programs appear to work better when specialized government agencies, such as the Student Financing Agency for Rwanda (SFAR), the HESLB in Tanzania, the SLTF in Ghana, and the Higher Education Loans Board (HELB) in Kenya, administer them and have formal relationships with other stakeholder institutions. While a separate loan agency was not created for the Ethiopian graduate tax, a well-codified set of administrative procedures divides specific administrative responsibilities among the Ministry of Education, the Federal Inland Revenue Authority and the academic institutions.

Nine, record keeping cannot adequately track borrowers. The collection records of student loan programs in Africa have been fairly dismal, and in some countries virtually no repayments have been collected. Nevertheless, this is changing for the better as governments recognize the importance of clear and robust collection systems. In Botswana, the Loans Recovery Service Division was recently created, and the ministry is planning to begin outsourcing student loan collection. The loan programs in Lesotho and Tanzania have also begun to use professional debt collection agencies to raise annual collection rates of outstanding repayments. In Kenya, HELB works with the credit bureau and the government tax authority to encourage compliance and track down defaulters. It also shares information with the National Social Security Fund and the Government Computer Centre. In Ethiopia, the Federal Inland Revenue Authority, the academic institutions, and employers play a role in loan collection under the oversight of the Ministry of Education.

Ten, economies provide too few jobs for the number of college and university graduates. Many of the loan programs have deferment and forbearance options for borrowers who are having problems repaying due to unemployment or other economic hardships. The HELB student loan program in Kenya, the grant-loan scheme in Botswana, and the National Student Financial Aid Scheme in Namibia have explicit deferment options. In Namibia, for example, a borrower who is unable to find employment within six months of completing his or her course can apply for a repayment extension. Moreover, a borrower who finds employment but is not earning a threshold salary may opt to pay back the loan without interest. Repayments may be suspended if the borrower becomes unemployed, has a salary that falls below the relevant threshold, or becomes disabled and unable to work. When the loan is suspended, no interest is accrued, although it begins to accrue again when repayment resumes. Other loan programs have limited deferment and forbearance options, which may push unemployed students into default. Ghana, Kenya, Lesotho, Malawi, Nigeria, and Tanzania all have fixed-schedule repayment obligations, while Burkina Faso, Ethiopia, Namibia, Rwanda, and South Africa have income-contingent repayment obligations.

2.7. Perceptions Toward Cost Sharing Policies

Studies on cost sharing say very little on the perception of stakeholders toward cost sharing policies. Obasi & Eboh (2002) studied students' views and perceptions on cost sharing. They reported that students were aware that the universities were grossly under-funded, had poor learning facilities and thus, required urgent financial attention. But, they were not in a position to accept the view that it is necessary to share the financial burden between them and other stakeholders.

Teshome (2003) reported stakeholders' perceptions of cost sharing in HEIs in Ethiopia. Based on reports of debates in many universities and the public debate on radio and newspapers conducted in 2002/2003 prior to the introduction of cost sharing in Ethiopia, Tehsome (2007) reported that the perceptions, opinions and reactions of both the public and the students to the introduction of cost sharing in Ethiopia were mixed. He wrote that "while many agreed to the principle of introducing cost sharing, they asked why it should be introduced at that particular time. He pointed out the reasons could be of personal interest (parental obligations, including to the would-be students) and partly because of pessimism about what the cost sharing would bring in terms of improving the higher education systems in terms of better quality, delivery and expansion" (p. 185).

Obasi and Eboh (2002) reported that the way education is financed affects students' and parents' perceptions of costs and benefits, and hence, determine private demand for education and cost sharing options. In their study on the perceptions of students and parents on cost sharing, Obasi & Eboh (2002) concluded that in Nigeria willingness to pay is a perception-ridden attribute that results from the interplay of an individual's worldview of university education (p. 34)

Tehsome (2007) noted the following perception of the students and the public in general with respect to cost sharing:

- Beneficiaries have to cover part of their cost of higher education and the services;
- Beneficiaries need to cover cost of higher education to ensure equitable redistribution of taxpayers' money;
- Cost sharing in the form of a graduate tax will level the field for both the affluent and the poor students, as all are required to pay back only after graduation;

- The repayments would bring some additional money to the treasury that would eventually be used to expand and improve the higher education sector improving access and opportunity;
- Cost sharing ease financial austerity of the government and enables to provide basic education, health services and other social services;
- Provision of education should be free and is the sole responsibility of the government as education is a public good.

Abdena (2005) concluded that students showed a positive attitude toward cost sharing in the Oromia regional colleges as high proportion of students expressed positive views towards the cost sharing scheme.

2.8. Cost Sharing Trends in Public HEIs

Cost sharing is a means to shift of the cost of higher education from government or taxpayers to students or their families. It is rapidly expanding to many countries in the world. As of 2007, about 13 African countries were charging higher education students one or the other form of cost of education in HEIs. Evidence from the World Bank report on cost sharing in Africa (2010) indicated that the implementation of cost sharing in Africa is expanding covering those Francophone countries that were reluctant to the notion of cost sharing as well as many Anglophone countries. As of 2009, at least 26 countries in Africa charge either tuition fees or other types of fees, such as examination fees, application fees, registration fees, identity card fees, library fees, and management information system fees (Caillaud, F. et al., 2009 and World Bank, 2010).

In many countries of the world, student loan programs are likely to be the most appropriate option for cost sharing where students and families do not have the capacity to pay fees at the time of study. Loans are the best option with the potential for providing finance and the advantage of passing the burden of cost sharing from current students or their families to working graduates (Asian Development Bank, 2009).

In the face of financial austerity and increasing enrolment in Ethiopia, cost sharing will continue as one of the government revenue generation sources. However, there will be a need to systematize and make efficient the revenue generation infrastructures for improving the cost recovery problem currently prevailing.

In summary, three types of cost sharing are implemented in Africa: upfront, deferred and dual track. Each of these types has a potential to supplement the government funding of HEIs. The upfront tuition fee scheme works where the parents can afford to pay the cost of their children's education and may be the best alternative in an affluent nation. In deferred schemes, students bear their cost of education which they are expected to pay after graduation in the form of loan or graduate tax. The effectiveness of such a scheme depends on the availability of jobs after graduation; follow up of graduates and the effectiveness of the collection of the payments. This scheme was implemented in a few African countries, including Ethiopia. The dual track scheme is common in East Africa particularly in Kenya, Tanzania and Uganda and is known for its improving access and the financial position of the HEIs. In the final analysis, there is no universal model of cost sharing scheme that could apply to all countries. Each country is obliged to adopt a system that fits its social policies and act accordingly.

3. Methods of the Study

3.1. Design of the Study

The design of the study was both quantitative and qualitative in its approach. Among the methods of quantitative approach, the survey method was employed for the study. For this kind of study, the survey method is the most appropriate. According to Creswell (2009), the survey method provides a quantitative or numeric description of trends, attitudes or opinions of a population by studying a sample of that population. Furthermore, Ary *et.al.* (2002) also stated that the survey method uses instruments, such as questionnaires and interviews, to gather information from a group of subjects. Surveys permit the researcher to summarize the characteristics of different groups or to measure their attitudes and opinions toward some issue (p. 25).

To obtain qualitative data, the study involved different groups of people. More specifically, individuals in charge of the cost-sharing scheme in the Ministry of Education, Ethiopian Revenues and Customs Authority, Addis Ababa and Adama universities were interviewed. Moreover, graduates (both males and females) of Adama and Addis Ababa universities who were involved in the cost-sharing scheme were interviewed to give their views. In addition to the interviews, relevant documents from the Ministry of Education, Ethiopian Revenues and Customs Authority, Addis Ababa and Adama universities and from graduates were obtained and analysed to answer the research questions. To integrate data obtained through quantitative and qualitative approach triangulation method was used.

3.2. Participants

The participants for the survey study were from two universities, namely: Addis Ababa and Adama. Questionnaires were distributed to a sample of 1500 students from the colleges/faculties of Social Sciences and Humanities, Business Education, Natural Sciences and Computational Sciences, Medicine and Health Sciences and Engineering and Technology. A total of 1048 students (78%) from the two universities completed and returned the questionnaires. The sample selection done for the study is presented in Table 5.

Table 5. Population and Sample of the Study

University	College/Faculty	Instructors				Students			
		Population		Sample		Population		Sample	
		N	%	N	%	N	%	N	%
Addis Ababa	Natural and Computational Sciences	143	34	17	17	1204	9	89	9
	Social Sciences and Humanities	337	78	39	39	7074	53	526	53
	Medicine and Health Sciences	151	36	18	18	1940	14	144	14
	Business and Economics	62	14	7	7	1629	12	121	12
	Engineering and Technology	163	38	19	19	1613	12	120	12
	Total	856	200	100	100	13460	100	1000	100
Adama	Natural and Computational Sciences	47	10	10	10	1560	24	118	24
	Social Science and Humanities	126	26	26	26	3228	48	244	48
	Engineering and Technology	302	64	64	64	1822	28	138	28
	Total	475	100	100	100	6610	100	500	100

Similarly, another set of questionnaires was distributed to 200 instructors from the Addis Ababa and Adama universities drawn from the colleges/faculties of Natural Sciences, Technology, Business and Economics, Education, Computer and Informatics and Teacher Education. A total of 123 instructors (62%) completed the questionnaire and returned. Stratified random sampling method was used to select the samples from both universities. Stratification was made separately within each faculty/college in each university based on the MoE (2009) education statistics annual abstract.

3.3. Instruments

In order to collect data, questionnaire and interview guides and secondary data collection formats were used for the study. The questionnaires were developed by the researchers and consisted of three parts. The first part was designed to collect demographic data and the second part consisted of scales to measure the perception of the students and instructors on the impact of cost sharing on quality of teaching and learning facilities in the universities under study. The third part of the questionnaire included questions on the extent of implementation, systems implemented, its effectiveness and challenges encountered in cost sharing scheme. Furthermore, interview guides were used to collect data from officers in charge of cost sharing in each university. In addition to this, another set of interview guide was designed to collect data from people working in the Ethiopian Revenues and Customs Authority who are dealing with the cost-sharing scheme and the graduates of the two universities who were involved in the cost sharing scheme. The major contents of the interview guides dealt with the impact of cost sharing on quality of teaching and learning, systems implemented, problems and challenges encountered at various levels.

3.4. Procedures

With a help of the letter secured from Forum for Social Studies (FSS), the two universities gave their consent to cooperate in the study. The validity and reliability of the instruments was ascertained through pilot testing and by critical comments made by experts. Pilot testing of the questionnaires was carried out on 50 students and instructors from Addis Ababa University. The questionnaires were edited and re-edited to improve their validity and accuracy. The reliability of the instrument for the scaled items was checked using Cronbach alpha method on the basis of the pilot data and found to be 0.82 for the students' questionnaire and 0.98 for the instructors' questionnaire, which are high and very high respectively for research instruments to be reliable (Cronbach, 1990).

Care was taken not to include in the final study the students who participated in the pilot testing of the instruments. Experts from FSS and Institute of Educational Research commented on the extent to which the questionnaires and interview guides could be used for the intended purpose. The questionnaire and interview guides were finalized by incorporating the comments of experts and data obtained through the pilot testing. Furthermore, formats were developed to collect secondary data related to cost sharing in HEIs. Finally, the questionnaires were distributed to students and instructors and collected after they have been filled out. The interviews were carried out at different times with different people related with the cost sharing scheme.

3.5. Methods of Data Analysis

In order to analyze the data obtained, appropriate methods and procedures were used in this study. The data obtained through questionnaires from students and instructors were entered into SPSS and checked for accuracy. From the data, appropriate statistics, such as percentages and descriptive statistics, were generated to answer the basic research questions. The data obtained from the interviews was transcribed and emerging themes were identified and analysed. Finally, all data obtained from the questionnaires, interviews and documents were triangulated in order to answer the basic research questions.

4. Data Presentation and Analysis

In this section, data collected from instructors and students in the campuses of the two universities during the time of data collection, graduates of Adama and Addis Ababa universities, cost-sharing officers of the two universities, as well as persons in charge of cost sharing offices in the Ministry of Education and in the Ethiopian Revenues and Customs Authority is presented. The data analysis is presented under five subsections namely: profile of respondents, instructors' level of teaching and class size, respondents' views concerning the introduction of cost sharing, impact of cost sharing on the provision of services and other related issues.

4.1. Profile of Respondents

In this study, the targeted sample size was 1500 undergraduate students (1000 students from Addis Ababa and 500 from Adama Universities) and 200 instructors (100 from Adama and 100 from Addis Ababa Universities). Questionnaires were distributed to a total of 1500 students and 200 instructors in both universities. The total number of responses obtained from both universities is shown in Table 6.

Table 6. Number of Respondents from the Addis Ababa and Adama universities

Respondents	University	N	%
Students	Addis Ababa University	565	53.9
	Adama University	466	44.5
	No Response	17	1.6
	Total	**1048**	**100.0**
Instructors	Addis Ababa University	59	48.0
	Adama University	64	52.0
	Total	**123**	**100.0**

It can be seen from Table 6 a total of 1048 (69.8%) students and 123 instructors (61.5%) filled out the questionnaire and returned. A total of 452 students (31%) and 77 instructors (38.5%) did not return the distributed questionnaires for various reasons. Table 6 also shows that 53.9% of the students who participated in this study were from Addis Ababa University while 44.5% were from Adama University. The other 1.6% of the respondents did not indicate their institutions. With regard to instructors, 48% were from Addis Ababa University and 52% were from Adama University

Table 7. Sex Composition of Students and Instructors

Respondents	Sex	N	%
Students	Male	790	75.4
	Female	234	22.3
	NR	24	2.3
	Total	1048	100.0
Instructors	Male	115	93.5
	Female	8	6.5
	Total	123	100.0

The sex composition of the students and instructors from both universities is shown in Table 7. Male students and instructors make up 75.4% and 93.5% of the respondents respectively while female students and instructors constituted for 22.3% and 6.5% of the respondents respectively. The other 2.3% of the students did not indicate their sexes. The sample students were chosen to reflect the proportion of males and females in undergraduate program at the national level. At the national level, the participation of girls at public institutions of higher learning is below 25% and that of the female instructors is below 9% (MoE, 2009). The data in Table 7 reflects similar pattern. The majority of the students attending the two universities belong to the age bracket of 20-24 (74.1%), followed by the group that belonged to age bracket 15-19 (19.3%). About 5% of the students were over the age of 25.

The instructors as well as students were also asked to indicate their respective faculties/colleges. This was done in order to show that the data was collected from diversified disciplines. As Table 8 shows, the respondents were from various faculties/colleges. The largest group is from technology (27.4%) followed by naturals sciences (24.6%). The third group comes from education (16.9) followed by medicine (12.6%)

The majority of the students who were involved in this study were second year students (35.2%). Third and first year students accounted for 28.6% and 25.9% of the total sample respectively. Fourth year and above are only 8.5%. Almost 2% of the respondents did not indicate their year of study.

Table 8. Distribution of Students and Instructors by Faculty/College

	Faculty/College	N	%
Students	Social sciences	47	4.5
	Faculty of business & economics	51	4.9
	Education	177	16.9
	Law	54	5.2
	Natural sciences	258	24.6
	School of Pharmacy	5	0.5
	Technology	287	27.4
	Medicine	132	12.6
	Pedagogy	18	1.7
	Others	1	0.1
	No response	18	1.7
	Total	**1048**	**100.0**
Instructors	Natural Sciences and Computational Sciences	15	12.20
	Engineering and Technology	26	21.14
	Faculty of Business Economics	13	10.57
	Social Sciences and Humanities	54	43.90
	No response	15	12.20
	Total	**123**	**100.00**

As can be observed from Table 8, the instructors from four faculties/colleges filled out and returned the questionnaire. The colleges/faculties included: Natural Sciences and Computational Sciences (12.20%), Engineering and Technology (21.14%), Faculty of Business Economics (10.57%), and Social Sciences and Humanities (43.90%). Instructors from the Faculty of Medicine and Health Sciences did not fill out and returned the questionnaire as planned.

Table 9. Educational qualification and academic rank of instructors

	Qualification	N	%
Qualification	BA/BSc	19	15.4
	MA/MSc	90	73.2
	PhD /MD/DVM	10	8.1
	Others	2	3.6
	No response	2	1.2
	Total	123	100.0
Academic Rank	Lecturer	75	61.0
	Assistant lecturer	16	13.0
	Assoc. Prof.	17	13.8
	Assist. Prof.	-	-
	Others	3	2.4
	No response	12	9.8
	Total	123	100.0

To indicate the profile of instructors is essential in this kind of study that involves tertiary level education. What they say about their teaching environment is important and it cannot be over looked. The majority of these instructors do have MA/MSc level qualifications (73.2%). Most of the instructors teach with the rank of lecturer (61.0%).

Table 10 has been constructed to examine what kind of services the students get as part of their cost-sharing scheme. As we can see in Table 10, the majority of the students (80.3%) get boarding and food services. Only 4.8% of students use food services while 4.7% of the students use boarding services. These variations in using university services by the students have implications on the cost sharing scheme. The implication is that those students who opted either for only food or boarding services will accumulate less debt at the end of their college education than those who use both food and boarding services.

Table 10. Types of services the students get as part of their cost sharing scheme

Service	N	%
Food	50	4.8
Boarding	49	4.7
Boarding and Food	842	80.3
Others	8	0.8
No Response	99	9.4
Total	1048	100.0

In higher education related studies where students are involved, it is usually reasonable to identify students' socio-economic status (SES). The main reason being that proportionally more students coming from urban areas and from well-to-do families usually attend institutions of higher learning as compared with those coming from lower socio-economic status as well as from rural areas. To ascertain such assumptions, proxy measures (such as students' parental education level and type of occupation) are used to estimate the SES (Tables 11 and 12).

Table 11. Students' Fathers and Mothers Educational Levels

Educational level	Fathers' Educational Level		Mothers' Educational Level	
	N	%	N	%
No any formal education	259	24.7	371	35.4
1-4 grades	127	12.1	129	12.3
5-8 grades	114	10.9	110	10.5
9-10 grades	51	4.9	71	6.8
11-12 grades	108	10.3	111	10.6
Diploma	129	12.3	117	11.2
BA/BSc Degree	139	13.3	66	6.3
MA/MSc Degree	32	3.1	10	1.0
Doctorate (PhD/ MD/MVD)	23	2.2	6	0.6
Others	2	0.2	1	0.1
No Response	64	6.1	56	5.3
Total	**1048**	**100.0**	**1048**	**100.0**

As can be seen from Table 11, 24.7% of the fathers and 35.4% of the mothers do not have any type of formal education. In terms of primary level of education (1-8 grades) the fathers and the mothers seem to be at par (i.e., 23% fathers and 22.8% mothers seem to have primary level education). When we look at secondary level education (9-12 grades), 17.4% of the students' mothers and 15.2% of the students' fathers do seem to have such levels of education. At the diploma level, 11, 2% of the mothers and 12.3% of the fathers seem to have such level of education. In this study, the mothers and fathers seem to have equal level of primary and secondary education. Table 11 also shows that the majority of the students attending both universities come from educated parents. A study reported by Sawyerr (2004) indicated that students attending tertiary level education in Mozambique, Uganda, Senegal, etc. were disproportionately represented from educated parents and this resulted in raising the question of access and equity at tertiary level education in Africa (p. 23).

Table 12. Students' Fathers and Mothers Occupation

Types of Occupation	Fathers' Occupation		Mothers' Occupation	
	N	%	N	%
Government Employee	240	22.9	151	14.4
Business person/self-employed	200	19.1	115	11.0
Farmer	387	36.9	237	22.8
Private employer	104	9.9	63	6.0
Daily labourer	13	1.2	10	1.0
House wife	-	-	438	41.8
Others	42	4.0	8	0.8
No Response	62	5.9	26	2.5
Total	**1048**	**100.0**	**1048**	**100.0**

The types of occupation in Table 12 can be categorized as non-farming occupation (government employee, business & self-employed and private employed), farming occupation, as well as, housewives and daily labourers. In view of this, almost 52% of the students' fathers and 31.4% of the mothers are engaged in non-farming occupations. One of the inherent characteristics of higher education is it caters more to the well-to-do and urban oriented segment of the population. Furthermore, about 37% of the fathers and almost 23% of the mothers are engaged in farming occupations. Close to 42% of the students' mothers are housewives. The percentage of parents categorized as daily labourers is few in numbers and therefore not worth mentioning.

It is a known fact that the majority of the Ethiopian population (85%) lives in rural areas. However, the majority of the students who complete their secondary education and join the institutions of public higher education come from urban areas. This is due to the fact that preparatory secondary schools (grades 11-12), are by and large located in urban areas and they accounted for 96.3% of urban secondary enrolment while rural preparatory secondary schools enrolment accounted for only 3.7% of the cohort (MoE, 2008). This bias towards the rural students is partly reflected in this study as Table 13 shows.

Table 13. Geographical location where students completed their secondary Preparatory education

Location	N	%
Urban	783	74.7
Rural	231	22.0
No Response	34	3.2
Total	**1048**	**100.0**

What we see in Table 13 is that almost 75% of the students indicated that they came from urban secondary preparatory schools. According to MoE (2009) in 2008 there were 952 secondary schools throughout the country. Out of these 952 secondary schools, 803 (84.3%) were located in urban areas and only 149 (15.7%) secondary schools were in rural areas. Because of this disparity between urban and rural secondary schools, students from urban areas have better opportunity to join the institutions of higher learning. According to Higher Education Proclamation No. 650/2009 (FDRE, 2009), one of the objectives of higher education is to ensure fairness in the distribution of public institutions and expand access on the basis of need and equity (p. 4979). However, the present study showed that most of the student respondents at AAU and AU were from: (1) urban areas (2) non-farming parents and (3) the three major ethnic groups specifically Amhara (38.9%), Oromo (31.4%) and Tigre (10.7%). Thus, the question of equity and access still remain to be addressed by the public institutions of higher learning.

It is worth mentioning at this juncture that the concept of student loans existed in Africa for more than 50 years. The first full-fledged loan programs were introduced in Ghana in 1971, Nigeria in 1973 and in Kenya in 1974. What has been ascertained so far is that cost sharing can bring new resources to higher education to expand capacity, improve quality and even expand accessibility and equity (World Bank, 2010).

Since there is financial austerity for expanding the public higher education sector, especially in countries like Ethiopia, it is believed logical that the beneficiaries share the cost of funding higher education. World Bank (2004) argued that from the point of equity, so far higher education is partaken by a very few and disproportionately by the children of more affluent parents and shifting the cost of higher education to citizens who can pay through direct or indirect taxation as beneficiaries. The World Bank also argued that cost sharing has a positive impact on the access, equity and efficiency of higher education, but in some instances, a difficult task to ascertain (World Bank, 2010)..

Marcucci & Johnstone (2007) also stated that the future trend of cost sharing regardless of one's personal perspective or ideological stance will continue as it is clear that there is a world-wide trend for decreased government support for higher education and increased costs for students and families in the form of some type of tuition fee. Furthermore, there is no "one best model" of cost-sharing that fits all countries with their specific traditions and political background. Hence, each country is well advised to review carefully to which degree its political objectives are actually fostered or indeed hampered by the cost-sharing system in place (Schwarzenberger, Opheim & Vibeke 2009).

Thus, the objectives of cost sharing are quite diversified according to the countries implementing it. For example, in an effort to improve students' completion rates, the National Student Financial Scheme of South Africa converts 40% of the loan to grant if the borrower performs well academically. In Botswana, the scheme is explicitly designed to influence program selection; and in Lesotho the cost-sharing scheme aims to influence post graduation behaviour in addition to its other objectives. It requires graduates who leave the country to pay back 100% of their tuition fees and living expenses (World Bank, 2010).

4. 2. Impact of Cost Sharing on Service Provisions

Past studies are not conclusive on the impact of cost sharing on the provision of services by higher education institutions. For example, studies show that cost sharing in Uganda's Makerere University, where the collection and utilization of the cost of education is the right of the university, it was reported that cost sharing has significantly increased access, efficiency and quality of services (Court, 1999). In Tanzania, students share cost through the loan system and the money recovered from cost sharing is not directly being utilized by the university, but deposited in central finance administration, and the impact of cost sharing in the improvement of resources was not visible (Mpiza, 2007).

In the Ethiopian situation, the Ethiopian Revenues and Customs Authority (ERCA), which is in charge of the cost-sharing scheme in accordance with the Income Tax Proclamation No. 154/2008, has the obligation to follow up, supervise and collect the total amount of payment to be made by the beneficiaries and deposit the collected amount directly in a government account specified for collecting the cost sharing revenue (Interview with ERCA Office, 2010). Thus, the money recovered from cost sharing does not reach directly the public higher education institutions so that they can supplement their regular budget.

However, the government of Ethiopia, through the ERCA, has been collecting loan repayments from the graduates of public higher education institutions for quite some time. Tables 14 and 15 show only the amount expected to be collected from the graduates of Addis Ababa and Adama Universities from 2005-2009. The only data available from the ERCA is the expected amount to be collected from graduates. ERCA has no complete data for the money collected so far from all graduates who participated in the cost-sharing scheme. Since graduates work (if they are employed/self employed) and live in different parts of the country, ERCA cannot collect all the repayment money by itself solely. In view of this, Higher Education Cost-sharing Regulation No.154/2008, article no. 6, states that: ERCA has the power to facilitate the collection of the graduate tax from beneficiaries from regional states and also article # 7 states that ERCA can delegate the power to collect cost-sharing payments to regional and municipality finance bureaus. Thus, the collection of the graduate tax is not a centralized activity and as the result it was not possible to get data on the total amount collected so far.

Table 14. Expected cost recovery from Addis Ababa University graduates (2008-2009)

Graduation year	No of Graduates	Expected Amount to be collected
2005	4074	32,126,516.57
2006	4588	43,642,909.15
2007	4761	48,844,412.43
2008	2910	34,241,568.92
2009	-	-
Total	16333	158,855,407.07

SOURCE: ERCA (2010)

Table 15. Expected cost recovery from Adama University graduates

Graduation year	No of Graduates	Expected Amount to be collected
2005	1289	10,088,640.96
2006	-	-
2007	1691	16,081,851.25
2008	1691	16,081,851.25
2009	2509	26,064,988.96
Total	7180	68,317,332.42

SOURCE: ERCA (2010).

The expected revenue that the government is going to collect from the graduates of public higher education institutions has been increasing as shown in Tables 14 and 15. The World Bank (2004) has stated the following on the Ethiopian cost-sharing scheme:

> Cost sharing, which is based on the current "graduate tax", is a positive step, but its impact will not be felt immediately because it takes a minimum of four years for enrolees to graduate and then start repaying through the proposed cost-sharing recovery scheme. If one assumes a tax of 10% of income for up to 15 years (as indicated in the Higher Education Cost-sharing Council of Ministers Regulation No. 154/2008), with some 35% of graduates exempt for various reasons, then cost-sharing would reduce the budget share of higher education in total public education spending by only 1 percentage point in 2008 or 2009. By the year 2020, the share for higher education in total education spending would be some 4 to 5 percentage points lower with cost-sharing than without. The income from cost sharing would represent a fairly reasonable 20% of the total cost of running the higher education system ... towards 2015 or 2020 (p. 23-24).

Cost sharing can bring new resources to higher education to expand capacity, improve quality and even accessibility and equity. But it can accomplish these things only (a) if governments (especially African governments) continue their current support for higher education using the potential new revenue from families and students to supplement rather than supplant or substitute, and (b) if financial assistance continues to be provided in the forms of means-tested (i.e. assessing the socio-economic situation of applicants and their families) grants based on parental income and student loans (World Bank, 2010, p. 77).

In this study, the instructors from Addis Ababa and Adama universities were asked if the introduction of cost sharing was the right decision. 83% of the instructors indicated that it was the right decision. Based on this response, Table 16 was constructed to show the opinion of instructors if there was any observed impact/change brought by cost-sharing (instructors are not usually expected to know all the details of their institutions' budget, but they are capable to give their opinions whether things are improving or going from bad to worse in their respective institutions) on the availability of various resources in their universities.

The opinions were measured using a five point of 1-5 scale (strong impact to very weak impact). On this scale, the expected average score is 3, which is the mid-point on the scale (Table 16). This opinion/attitude scale is based on the Likert method. The attitude/opinion scale determines what an individual believes, perceives, or feels about self, others, and a variety of activities, institutions, and situations (Gay & Airasian, 2000, p.156). The Likert scale is one of the most widely used techniques to measure attitudes/opinions (Ary, et.al. 2002). The first step in constructing a Likert scale is to collect a number of statements on a subject. The correctness of the statements is not important as long as they express opinions held by a substantial number of people. The simplest way to describe opinion is to indicate percentage responses for each individual statement (Best & Khan, 2005, p. 318). Thus, Table 16 is constructed based on the justifications stated above.

Table 16. *The extent cost sharing brought impact on teaching and learning by making facilities available*

Type of Service	Very weak impact		Weak impact		Some impact		Very strong impact		Strong impact		Average
	N	%	N	%	N	%	N	%	N	%	
Availability of textbooks	30	24.4	22	17.9	27	22.0	22	17.9	8	6.5	2.60
Having reasonable number of students per class	46	37.4	24	19.5	9	7.3	25	20.3	6	4.9	2.28
Having enough reference materials	32	26.0	26	21.1	30	24.4	17	13.8	6	4.9	2.45
Provision of journals	44	35.8	27	22.0	19	15.4	12	9.8	8	6.5	2.21
Provision of libraries	29	23.6	26	21.1	27	22.0	23	18.7	5	4.1	2.54
Availability of reading rooms	33	26.8	32	26.0	27	22.0	14	11.4	5	4.1	2.33
Availability of computers	24	19.5	28	22.8	26	21.1	27	22.0	6	4.9	2.67
Access to internet services	25	20.3	28	22.8	26	21.1	24	19.5	8	6.5	2.66
Availability of laboratory equipments	31	25.2	30	24.4	23	18.7	17	13.8	6	4.9	2.41
Availability of washrooms	52	42.3	24	19.5	19	15.4	13	10.6	2	1.6	1.99
Staff offices	48	39.0	25	20.3	16	13.0	19	15.4	2	1.6	2.11
Photocopy and printing services	34	27.6	28	22.8	23	18.7	21	17.1	5	4.1	2.41
Overall average											**2.34**

As shown in Table 16, the overall opinion of instructors on the impact of cost sharing on the teaching/learning process by making various resources available inclined towards "weak impact" as the overall average is 2.34. The instructors were of the opinion that cost sharing has very weak impact on the availability of washrooms (42.3%), staff offices (39.0%), having reasonable number of students per class (37.4%) and provision of journals (35.8%).

Table 17 presents the expectation of instructors from the cost sharing scheme in improving the quality of various services in their universities. Their expectations were measured by a three-point scale from low to high (1 = low, 2 = moderate and 3 = high)

Table 17. Expected qualities of facilities/services as the result of cost sharing scheme

Type of Service	High		Moderate		Low		$\overline{X}$
	N	%	N	%	N	%	
Internet	31	25.2	41	33.3	37	30.1	2.06
Library services	23	18.7	53	43.1	33	26.8	2.09
Textbooks	25	20.3	45	36.6	39	31.7	2.13
Classrooms	22	17.9	37	30.1	50	40.7	2.26
Washing rooms	11	8.9	42	34.1	56	45.5	2.41
Cafeteria	23	18.7	40	32.5	46	37.4	2.21
Counselling	17	13.8	37	30.1	55	44.7	2.35
Health	22	17.9	45	36.6	42	34.1	2.18
Recreation	13	10.6	48	39.0	48	39.0	2.32
Information	26	21.1	43	35.0	39	31.7	2.12
Sport facilities	18	14.6	53	43.1	46	37.4	2.24
Laboratory (if applicable)	17	13.8	36	29.3	59	48.0	2.38
References and other reading materials	28	22.8	38	30.9	51	41.5	2.20
Overall mean							**2.22**

As indicated in Table 17, the expectation of instructors with regard to the impact of cost sharing on the quality of various services is moderate with a mean score of 2.22 on a three point scale designed to measure the qualities of services as a result of cost sharing.

As beneficiaries, higher education students enter into contract agreement with their institutions through the cost-sharing scheme. Once they sign the agreement they are entitled for the services that the institutions provide. These services are expected to meet the needs of the students. In regard to this, the World Bank (1997) indicated that:

> Financial contributions toward the cost of their education by a significant portion of university students can enhance educational quality and relevance. When students pay something for their education, they are likely to generate pressures for increased accountability on the part of academic staff and administrators. Fee-paying students are more likely to oblige academic staff to attend class, to come prepared, and to be available for student consultations. They will be concerned with the connection between what they learn and their future income-earning possibilities. They are also likely to be motivated to complete their studies in good time, thus improving the internal efficiency of the educational institutions (p. 12).

In view of this, the students were asked to indicate the quality of services they expected from their institutions as signatories of the cost-sharing scheme. The responses of the students are shown in Table 18.

Table 18. *Extent of the quality of services students expected as a result of cost sharing scheme*

Type of Service	High		Moderate		Low		Total	
	N	%	N	%	N	%	N	%
Internet	481	45.9	294	28.1	220	21.0	995	94.9
Library services	594	56.7	311	29.7	92	8.8	997	95.1
Textbooks	416	39.7	344	32.8	235	22.4	995	94.9
Classrooms	481	45.9	358	34.2	144	13.7	983	93.8
Rest room (Wash room)	314	30.0	359	34.3	306	29.2	979	93.4
Cafeteria	348	33.2	378	36.1	259	24.7	985	94.0
Dormitory	464	44.3	350	33.4	164	15.6	978	93.3
Counselling	246	23.5	342	32.6	385	36.7	973	92.8
Health	327	31.2	339	32.3	323	30.8	989	94.4
Recreation	234	22.3	344	32.8	399	38.1	977	93.2
Information	383	36.5	378	36.1	231	22.0	992	94.7
Sport facilities	220	21.0	350	33.4	412	39.3	982	93.7
Laboratory (if applicable)	326	31.1	311	29.7	298	28.4	935	89.2
References and other reading materials	406	38.7	361	34.4	216	20.6	983	93.8

What we see in Table 18 is that most students in both universities had either high or moderate expectations of the services when they joined these universities. Then these students were again asked to rate the services they get currently while pursuing their education. The students' ratings are shown below in Table 19.

Table 19. Extent of the quality of services students currently getting from their universities

Type of Service	High		Moderate		Low		Total	
	N	%	N	%	N	%	N	%
Internet	369	35.2	304	29.0	264	25.2	937	89.4
Library services	363	34.6	413	39.4	169	16.1	945	90.2
Textbooks	191	18.2	383	36.5	358	34.2	932	88.9
Classrooms	254	24.2	444	42.4	235	22.4	933	89.0
Rest room (Wash room)	127	12.1	356	34.0	444	42.4	927	88.5
Cafeteria	153	14.6	411	39.2	358	34.2	922	88.0
Dormitory	255	24.3	384	36.6	281	26.8	920	87.8
Counselling	79	7.5	310	29.6	531	50.7	920	87.8
Health	98	9.4	371	35.4	455	43.4	924	88.2
Recreation	80	7.6	316	30.2	528	50.4	924	88.2
Information	192	18.3	394	37.6	348	33.2	934	89.1
Sport facilities	78	7.4	318	30.3	532	50.8	928	88.5
Laboratory (if applicable)	124	11.8	328	31.3	416	39.7	868	82.8
References and other reading materials	200	19.1	384	36.6	328	31.3	912	87.0

Table 19 has been constructed in order to see clearly students' rating of the quality of services that they get from their universities. When we take a closer look at services that are rated as either high or low by the students the following picture emerges as shown in Table 19. What we see in Table 19 is that 35% of the students rated the quality of internet and library as high. Then a little over 24% rated dormitory and classrooms services as high. Furthermore, between 18-19% of the students rated the quality of reference/reading materials, information, and textbooks, and cafeteria services as high. In addition to this, over 50% of the students rated services related to sport facilities, counselling and recreation facilities as low. Furthermore, between 33.2-43.4% of the students also rated health services, washrooms, laboratories, cafeteria, textbooks as well as information services as low.

Table 20: Services rated as high or low by cost sharing students from Addis Ababa and Adama universities (as shown in ranking order).

High Rated Services	% of students	Rank	Low Rated Services	% of Students
Internet	35.2	1	Sport facilities	50.8
Library	34.6	2	Counselling	50.7
Dormitory	24.3	3	Recreation facilities	50.4
Class Rooms	24.2	4	Health services	43.4
References/reading materials	19.1	5	Washrooms/toilets	42.4
Information services	18.3	6	Laboratories	39.7
Textbooks	18.2	7	Cafeteria and textbooks	34.2
Cafeteria	14.6	8	Information services	33.2

Finally, students were asked to indicate their overall ratings of the quality of services they get from their respective universities. The overall ratings of the students are shown in Table 21.

Table 21. Students rating of the services they get currently from their universities considering what they will pay as a graduate tax

Responses	N	%
High	414	39.5
Moderate	534	51.0
No Response	100	9.5
Total	1048	100

As can be seen from Table 21, 51% of the students rated the services they get from their universities as moderate. Almost 40% of the students rated the services they get as high. Less than 10% of the students did not respond to the questionnaire.

So far data obtained mainly from students who were pursuing their studies at Addis Ababa and Adama universities during the time of data collection were discussed. What follows next is the analysis of the data obtained from MOE education statistics abstracts and different stakeholders, namely: those who graduated (beneficiaries) after the introduction of cost sharing in 2003/04, the Ministry of Education, the Ethiopian Revenues and Customs Authority and the two universities involved in this study.

=Since the introduction of the cost-sharing scheme in 2003/04, thousands of students have graduated from the public institutions of higher learning and joined the labour market. Our study focused only on those who graduated from regular undergraduate programs of Addis Ababa and Adama Universities. Table 22 shows the number of graduates from 2003/04-2008/09 and the estimated amount of cost to be recovered from the graduates.

Table 22. Graduates from Public Higher Education Institutions and estimated cost recovery (2003/04-2008/09.

Year	Undergraduate Regular	Average cost per training year*	Average training year*	Estimated amount to be recovered
2003/04	4965	4351.022	3.625	78310237.83
2004/05	7380	4351.022	3.625	116400716.1
2005/06	21472	4351.022	3.625	338666148.4
2006/07	23367	4351.022	3.625	368554950.1
2007/08	26839	4351.022	3.625	423316913
2008/09	31926	4351.022	3.625	503551390.3

SOURCE: MOE (2009)

* The estimation is based on the data from Table 26.

As shown in Table 22, assuming that there will be no default in the cost recovery from graduates, it is estimated that the amount of recovery would be Birr 78,310, 237 from the graduates of the academic year 2003/04 and would reach Birr 503, 551, 390 from the graduates of the academic year 2008/09.

Data on the number of graduates and the revenue expected to be collected from universities were not available for all universities, as the graduates from new universities have not yet reported to ERCA. The data below shows the number of graduates and the revenue expected to be collected from five universities during the period 2005/06 to 2009/10.

Table 23. Graduates and expected revenue to be collected by universities (2005/06 to 2009/10)

University	Graduates	Amount to be collected
Haramaya University	19,375	156,086,882.79
Addis Ababa University*	16,333	158, 855,407.07
Hawassa University*	6,511	51,270,801
Adama University**	7,180	68,317,332.48
Jimma University*	12, 373	107,741,231.69
Total	**61,772**	**383,416,247.96**

SOURCE: Ethiopian Revenues and Customs Authority

* No data for 2009/10

** No data for 2006/07

As seen from Table 23, during the last five years a total of Birr 383, 416, 247.96 was expected to be collected from the five universities for which the data is available. Data was not available at the ERCA on how much of this amount was collected.

In order to give legal base for the aforementioned stakeholders, the government enacted proclamation No. 154/2008. This proclamation spelt out the duties and responsibilities of each stakeholder as summarized in Table 24 (See Annex 1 for details of the Proclamation).

Table 24. A Brief summary of basic facts related to cost- sharing scheme

Services	Estimated cost	Remark
Food	100%; the cost has been revised twice by MOE since the introduction of cost sharing as indicated in Table 25 below.	Cost change could be effected only by the directives of MOE
Boarding	100%; the cost has not been revised since the introduction of cost sharing as indicated in Table 25 below.	Cost change could be effected only by the directives of MOE
Tuition	15% of the total cost	Each institution is entitled to make cost adjustments based on yearly budget and guidelines of MOE
Total	Food, boarding and tuition fee	All debt must be paid within 15 years time after graduation

Table 24 was constructed to show how the cost-sharing scheme has been implemented since 2003/04 throughout the public institutions of higher learning. The guidelines issued by the MoE (2009) specify how tuition fee and cost of food and boarding are set. It specifies that the beneficiaries should share (a) total cost of cafeteria, (b) total accommodation cost, and (c) not less than 15% of the administrative costs directly related to education and training. The costs the beneficiaries should not share were specified as cost of (a) reception, (b) plant, machinery and material maintenance, (c) domestic trainings (c) purchase of vehicles and others, (d) building materials and (e) salary of workers who are working in the income generating sections (pp. 2-3). An exception to this regulation is that of medical students who pay full cost of their training with a penalty of 50% if they default to provide services in the government health institutions for a specified period of time.

Costs that were directly related to education and training were defined as (a) 20% of the salary of the current working instructors (b) 15% of the salary of instructors who are on study leave training and sabbatical leave, (c) 20% of the salary of technical assistance and laboratory workers and 20% of salary of expatriate teachers (MoE, 2009).

Table 25. Students boarding and food fees from 2005/06-2009/10*

Year	Boarding	Food	Total
2005/06	600	1200	1800
2007/08	600	1800	2400
2009/10	600	2400	3000

* NOTE: Cost-sharing scheme includes food, boarding and tuitions. The directives of the Ministry of Education dictate the cost of food and boarding. Each institution decides its own tuition fees, which varies from time to time and also within various faculties/colleges in the same university.

As can be observed in Table 25, since the introduction of cost sharing, the costs of boarding did not change. Due to changing market prices, the cost of food was revised twice in 2007 and 2009. In 2005/06, the cost for food was 120 Birr per month, then in 2007/08 it was 180 Birr per month and in 2009/10 the cost reached 240 Birr per month. Each university sets the cost of tuition for its own students. Accordingly, the following Tables 26 and 27 were constructed to show the costs of boarding, food and tuition fees of the two universities.

Table 26. Cost sharing fees by field of study at Addis Ababa University (2009/10)

Field of Study	Program Year	Food	Boarding	Tuition	Total
Business and Economics	3	2400	600	1377.12	4377.12
Dental	4	2400	600	2871.08	5871.08
Education	3	2400	600	944.30	3944.30
Fine Arts and Design	4	2400	600	1766.19	4766.19
Informatics	3	2400	600	998.75	3998.75
Journalism and Communication	3	2400	600	1370.57	4370.57
Laboratory Technology	4	2400	600	979.63	3979.63
Language Studies	3	2400	600	909.22	3909.22
Law	4	2400	600	811.80	3811.80
Medicine	5.5	2400	660	2490.51	5550.51
Music	5	2400	600	2079.54	5079.54
Natural Sciences	3	2400	600	847.18	3847.18
Nursing/Midwifery Diploma	2	2400	600	1072.68	4072.68
Nursing Degree	4	2400	600	1556.97	4556.97
Pharmacy	4	2400	600	835.42	3835.42
Social Sciences	3	2400	600	625.95	3625.95
Technology (North)	4	2400	600	1382.11	4382.11
Technology (South) degree	4	2400	600	1272.12	4272.12
Technology (South) diploma	3	2400	600	646.20	3646.20
Veterinary Medicine	4	2400	600	2123.10	5123.10
Average	**3.625**	**2400**	**600**	**1348.02**	**4351.02**

SOURCE: Addis Ababa University, Cost sharing Office

The cost sharing fee has three components: food, boarding and tuition. Irrespective of the students' field of study, the cost of food and boarding are the same except for the Faculty of Medicine, which is different due to the duration of the study, i.e. 11 months in a year. In reality, if medicine graduates default on providing services in government institutions for specified terms required of them, they are obliged to pay the full cost of their education and 50% penalty to release their diploma. The tuition cost is determined every year and varies by fields of study. In 2009/10, the highest cost sharing was that of the dental students which was 5871.08 Birr; the second highest was that of medical students which was 5550.51 Birr and the third highest fee was that of veterinary students which was 5123.10 Birr. The three fields of study for the degree programs with least amount of cost sharing for the 2009/10 at Addis Ababa University were social sciences (3646.20 Birr), law (3811.80 Birr) and Pharmacy (3835.42 Birr).

Adama University is one of the new institutions of higher learning located in Adama town. The university has six major divisions called "Schools". They are:

- School of Agriculture (located in Assela)
- School of Health (located in Assela)
- School of Business Administration, Management and Trade (located in Adama)
- School of Engineering and Information Technologies (located in Adama)
- School of Humanities and Natural Sciences (located in Adama)
- School of Pedagogic and Vocational Teacher Education (located in Adama)

The data for this study covered only those schools located in Adama town.

Table 27. *Cost sharing fees by field of study at Adama University (2009/10)*

Schools/Colleges	Program Year	Food	Boarding	Tuition fee per credit hours
School of Engineering and Information Technology	5	2400	600	23.61
School of Business administration, Management and Trade	3	2400	600	9.58
School of Pedagogical and Vocational Education	3	2400	600	9,58
School of Humanities and Natural Science	3	2400	600	9,58

As shown in Table 27, courses in engineering and in sciences that require laboratory facilities are more expensive than others. The tuition fee for the School of Engineering and Information Technology is 23.61 Birr/credit hours whereas the tuition for the schools of School of Business Administration, Management and Trade, School of Pedagogical and Vocational Education and School of Humanities and Natural Sciences is 9.58 Birr/credit hour.

When a student completes his/her studies, the institution has the obligation to provide the beneficiary with necessary information and documents related to the amounts of cost sharing owed by him/her upon leaving the institution (Article 12 of the Regulation No. 154/2008). The beneficiary has also the obligation to pay back his/her debt according to the agreement made with the institution.

4.3 Qualitative Data Analysis

In order to see how the cost-sharing money is being recovered as well as its implementation process, various interviews were carried out with the following stakeholders, namely: the beneficiaries (the graduates), the ministry of education, personnel from Addis Ababa and Adama Universities in charge of the cost-sharing office and the Ethiopian Revenues and Customs Authority,

Before going into the details of the interview, it is deemed necessary to indicate the significance of the Higher Education Cost-sharing Council of Ministers Regulation No.154/2008. The specific articles enumerated in this regulation make it clear the duties and responsibilities of the following stakeholders (for details see Annex 1): The articles are:

1. Article 7 (in reference to employers).
2. Article 8 (in reference to beneficiaries)
3. Article 10 (in reference to the MoE)
4. Article 11 (in reference to ERCA)
5. Article 12 (in reference to the HEIs)

As a matter of procedure, the names of the people interviewed will be kept anonymous. Instead of reporting the interview responses separately, it was found to be desirable to summarize them within the following categories: (a) graduates (b) officers in charge of cost-sharing scheme at Addis Ababa and Adama universities, (c) the Ethiopian Revenues and Customs Authority and (d) the Ministry of Education.

A. Graduates from the Addis Ababa and Adama Universities.

Four graduates (one male and three females) were interviewed to give their experiences concerning cost sharing. The male graduate signed his contract agreement in 2005 and graduated in 2006. He accumulated a debt (food and boarding) of 1800 Birr and a tuition fee of 15%. He started paying his graduate tax of 10% (56 Birr/month) soon after being employed and hopes to finish his debt in 15 years time. In this connection the B1 (beneficiary 1) stated that:

> I have started paying my graduate tax just after I was employed. I started to pay 10% of my salary. I used to pay 56 Birr per month. I paid for one year when I was in the Finance Department. However, I stopped paying when I transferred to a different department within the same organization. Then, I transferred from the second department to another third department. During my transfers from the first to the second or to the third department, I was not asked to continue to pay the graduate tax by the organization that employed me.

The beneficiaries know that a graduate tax is a debt that should be paid some day. However, an interview with a beneficiary indicates that at least all of them do not know that they will be required to pay the graduate tax with interest. An interview with a beneficiary shows that some of the beneficiaries were not aware that a graduate tax includes interest. In an interview, B1 responded that:

"I know that a graduate tax is my debt. But I do not pay interest because I did not sign the contract to pay interest. It is free of interest."

On the other hand, there are beneficiaries who know that cost sharing is a debt on which interest is paid. In this regard B2 said that:

> "I have to pay upfront my cost sharing fee to get my documents and a discount of 5%". I know if not paid it is my debt that includes interest. Therefore, it is better to pay upfront the cost that I agreed to share for my education."

According to this graduate, the 10% graduate tax that the government imposed and to be collected every month from the graduates is very high. In reference to this 10% graduate tax, the World Bank Sector Study (2004) stated that the minimum tax rate is set to 10%. This is a very large by international standards, and especially so in a low-come country (p. 24). Also, the beneficiary cannot get any exemption from graduate tax because he is not working in the areas of health or education.

The issue of affordability is important for those who pay proper graduate tax and totally rely on their salary for every expense. In this regard, one of the beneficiaries interviewed (B_1) said that:

> "For me payment of graduate tax in not affordable. Nowadays the rent of a house and living expenses have tremendously increased and made it very

difficult to pay 10% of my salary as a graduate tax. That is also one of the reasons I did not continue to pay upon my transfer from one department to the other."

The three female graduates who participated in this interview came from different backgrounds. Two of them went to Nazareth Girls' School and joined the Faculty of Business and Economics, Addis Ababa University (AAU). They had no financial problems while attending their education at AAU. While at AAU, they did not use food and boarding, but only collected a sum of Birr 300/month, and each of them accumulated a total debt of Birr 13,131.36 at the time of their graduation. During the interview, they explained that they were ready to repay their debt (with the help of their parents) at once and get a 3% discount on their debt in accordance with Proclamation No.286/2002; and also claim their diplomas. The 300 birr/month that they used to get from AAU finance office was spent on transportation, photocopying, and on other personal expenses.

The third female student who graduated from Adama University in 2007 completed her secondary education at a government high school. She studied business education for three years and accumulated a debt of Birr 6435. She used food and boarding and 15% tuition fee. She went into teaching and expects to pay back her debt rendering three years of teaching service (Regulation No. 154/2008). Due to her parental economic situation as well as hers, she could not settle her debt at once like the other two female students from Addis Ababa University who were able to settle their debt as soon as they graduated. What was observed in this study was that graduates coming from different backgrounds do use cost sharing scheme in different ways. Those who live with their parents get in cash the fee earmarked for food and boarding and use the cash for personal expenses while others who stay within the campus get food and boarding services only.

B. Officers in Charge of Cost Sharing at Addis Ababa and Adama Universities.

They were interviewed to know how the implementation of cost sharing works in their respective institutions.

Addis Ababa University is a big institution with a large student population enrolled in various colleges/departments and disciplines. As a result, there are variations in costs that students are subjected to (see Table 26). The person in charge of the cost-sharing scheme pointed out that:

> "The amount of cost sharing is determined by dividing the sum of the recurrent budget and overhead cost by the total number of students plus 50 Birr for medical coverage. This is determined by each faculty. In a faculty/college where there are less number of students the tuition fee is high."

The three departments/faculties with the highest amount of cost-sharing fee are: Dental, Medicine and Yared Music School. The reason for this high amount is due to the cost of laboratory materials, teaching equipments/ instruments, etc. It was also indicated that since boarding is not allowed for students from Addis Ababa, the following problems have been observed: Even though the exact number is unknown, a large number of students live far away from AAU campus. Due to the high cost of transportation and problems associated with it, some come to class late or miss classes altogether. This situation results in inconvenience and frustration. Consequently, the academic performances of some of the students have been affected and finally this led some to drop out. This problem still persists.

The situation at Adama University is mostly related to the problems of administration and management of cost sharing. Almost all the students live within the campus. The amount of cost sharing varies according to areas of speciality (Table 27).

C. The Ministry of Education

The Ministry of Education is one of the key players in the design, implementation and follow up of the cost-sharing scheme. Article 10 of the Regulation No. 154/2008 delineated the powers and duties of the Ministry of Education. The Ministry has a huge responsibility in the cost sharing scheme and the person in charge indicated that:

> "Two groups determine cost sharing: the House of Peoples' Representatives and the universities. The House of Peoples' Representatives determines the food and dormitory costs and the universities determine the 15% tuition fee. Each university determines the tuition fee to be paid by students from each faculty. This is determined each year at the beginning of the academic calendar."

Furthermore, the person indicated that:

> The stakeholders' of the cost-sharing scheme also included: the Ministry of Education, the Ethiopian Revenues and Customs Authority, HEIs, the beneficiaries, Ministry of Health, Ministry of Justice and employers. The Ministry of Education is responsible for the development of policies and guidelines on cost sharing and the Ministry of Justice is responsible for the implementation of the cost-sharing bylaws and regulations. The HEIs are responsible for entering students in cost-sharing agreement contracts, sending

the list of students after they entered agreements, and also the list of graduates to the Ethiopian Revenues and Customs Authority every year after graduation. In this scheme, no program is waived from cost sharing. Students enter into an agreement to pay their graduate tax either in cash or through rendering service. Students who join teaching and health fields, where there are shortages of educated manpower, pay their debts by rendering services for each training year and the other graduates pay their graduate tax in cash. Students in this area, i.e. teaching and health, if they do not want to provide services, they are liable to pay all outstanding cost of their education with additional penalty of 50% of their outstanding cost.

He further noted that so far a number of problems have been observed in the implementation of the cost sharing policy. One of the major problems is students discontinuing their education because of inability to cope with challenges of higher education. Discontinuing education at the middle of a program is a great loss in terms of cost sharing. There is no other way to collect costs of their education from such students. Such students also make requests for their documents as they need them for employment. The MoE Official further noted that the Ministry of Education provides documents for such students if they could produce a guarantee. Another problem is with graduates who were employed in private organizations. Some of these organizations do not enforce the payment of graduate tax and in fact consider it as an incentive for the employees to stay in the organization.

The person in charge also reiterated that the Ministry of Education does not consider it as a violation of the rights of the beneficiaries by withholding their diploma where an agreement was made. If the beneficiaries fail to fulfill their duties of providing services for the period expressed in the agreement, then they are liable for their actions. Withholding graduates' diplomas was found to have no effect in terms of job search as graduates are given temporary certificates that would help them in job search. However, during the interview those graduates who wanted to join graduate programs or attend further training were asked to settle their debt in full before joining such programs. Government sponsored students who want to join graduate programs do not experience such problems.

D. The Ethiopian Revenues and Customs Authority

The ERCA has the responsibility to collect the graduate tax from all graduates of Public HEIs. During the course of this study it was found that:

1. Taking into account Article 11, Regulation No.154/2008, ERCA developed a guideline that outlines the major activities to be taken in regard to collecting the graduate tax.
2. Graduates are already paying their "graduate taxes" as part of their obligation. The official from the ERCA said in this regard there are significant number of beneficiaries who are paying their cost sharing at various places designated for this purpose. The places are regional and woreda finance bureaus for Addis Ababa.
3. ERCA is attempting to strengthen the link between the universities.

    In this regard, an official from ERCA said that "currently we are planning to strengthen our link with universities so that we can get up to date on beneficiaries who entered cost sharing agreement, who have withdrawn or discontinued their education and who graduated at the end."
4. ERCA deposits the collected graduate tax money in a special account designated by the Ministry of Finance and Economic Development. However, the amount of money collected so far from the graduate tax has not been calculated and known. According to the official from ERCA "this is mainly due to the fact that the unit is understaffed and lacks a modern working system."
5. As the number of universities increase in the future so does the number of graduates. Things cannot go on forever as they are now. Thus, the unit that handles the cost-sharing activities must expand to serve beneficiaries from these universities well.
6. ERCA is considering decentralizing its activities to regional states and other relevant organizations to be more efficient, accountable and transparent. This intention to decentralize would be useful for timely cost recovery from beneficiaries and follow in case they of default on obligations.

5. Summary and Recommendations

5.1. Summary

The major purpose of this study was to investigate various aspects of cost-sharing scheme. The participants of the study were students and instructors from Addis Ababa and Adama universities, officers in charge of cost-sharing units in each of the two universities, graduates from the two institutions, Ministry of Education and also the Ethiopian Revenues and Customs Authority. Data were collected from these sources using various data collecting instruments and analyzed qualitatively and quantitatively. The following summary points were derived from the major findings of this study.

In the Ethiopian context, the introduction of cost sharing in 2003/04 is a recent phenomenon as compared with many other African countries and the system is not fully developed as it should have been. Even though many countries in the world apply cost sharing in their higher institutions of learning, there is no universal model that could apply to all countries. Each country is obliged to adopt a system that fits its social policies and implement it accordingly.

There are three types of commonly known tuition fees that are practiced in cost sharing schemes: Namely; up-front, dual track and deferred. Ethiopia uses the deferred system in the form of a graduate tax scheme. Nine of the thirteen loan programs in Africa use means-testing (i.e. assessing the socio-economic situation of applicants and their families) in the awarding of loans. Only Ethiopia, Lesotho and Swaziland use deferred payment of cost sharing scheme to all higher education students. Ethiopia charges 10% graduate tax as means of collecting loan repayments from all graduates. This is considered as too high as compared with other African countries.

In Ethiopia, the cost sharing scheme involves higher education institutions, the students and their families, ERCA, the Ministry of Education as well as the employers. In this study, it has been observed that the involvement of many stakeholders has complicated the collection of revenues from the graduates. Many African countries have systematized the means of collecting revenues from their graduates and these collected revenues are re-channeled to the coffers of higher education institutions. This is not the case in the Ethiopian situation.

It is strongly believed that cost sharing could bring new resources to higher education to expand capacity, bring equity, and improve quality as well as accessibility. In this study, the impact of cost sharing in improving the teaching/learning process in Ethiopian higher education institutions has not been strongly ascertained.

5.2. Recommendations

The following recommendations were made on the basis of the findings of the study.

1. The study revealed that the students as well as the instructors in both universities accepted the reality of cost sharing. What they could not see was its direct link and impact on resource generation in relation to their institutions. In some African countries, the revenue collected from graduates goes back to their former institutions. This approach helps to supplement the budget of the institution in addition to what the government allocates. This approach has to be considered seriously by the government.

2. The offices in charge of cost-sharing scheme in the two universities, Ministry of Education or the Ethiopian Revenues and Customs Authority lack qualified staff and resources to deliver efficient services to those who need it. These deficiencies need to be rectified.

3. The graduates indicated that the 10% graduate tax is quite high taking into account the constantly rising cost of living. The government has to reconsider the amount of graduate tax that is being paid in comparison with other similar African countries.

4. All graduates are expected to pay a 10% graduate tax whatever their monthly or yearly income happens to be. The percentage of graduate tax must be contingent on the person's income. Being employed after graduation does not mean to have a good income, especially for the young. To make this work there must be a good data base on graduates.

5. The study also revealed that the overall system link between the universities and the Ethiopian Revenue and Customs Authority is not well established for better information and data exchange. This has to be improved to make the system more efficient and full proof.

6. Withholding diplomas of graduates from various fields of studies is seen as an outdated act. Instead of withholding diplomas of graduates, the government has to devise various incentive method/mechanism (reasonable compensation, better working environment, etc.,) to attract and retain qualified professionals.

7. The number of graduates from public higher institutions of learning is increasing every year and the current system cannot cope up with the future volume of work. Attention must be given to handle the future volume of work. In order to handle the growing volume of work in the

future, there must a separate and independent body/office outside the ERCA. A number of African countries do have separate offices that handle the collection of student loans.
8. This study has been carried out on the two universities only. In the future, a large comprehensive nationwide study is needed to see the impact of cost sharing in enhancing the teaching-learning process.

References

Abdena Angos Segni (2005). *Attitude of Students towards Cost sharing in Oromiya Regional Colleges*. Masters Thesis, Addis Ababa University.

Abebayehu A., Tekleselassie and Johnstone D. B. (2004). *Means Testing: The Dilemma of Targeting Subsidies in African Higher Education.* JHEA/RESA, 2(2), 135–158

Adams, A. V. and Hartnett T. (1996). *Cost Sharing in the Social Sectors of Sub-Saharan Africa: Impact on the Poor.* The World Bank discussion paper No. 338. Washington D.C. The World Bank.

African Region Human Development (2004). Working paper series - No. 66. Accra, Ghana.

Albrecht, D. and Ziderman, A. (1991). *Deferred Cost Recovery for Higher Education: Student Loan Programs in Developing Countries.* The World Bank.

Ary, D., Jacobs, L. C. & Razavieh, A. (2002). *Introduction to Research in Education.* 6th ed. United States: Wadsworth.

Asian Development Bank. (2009). *Good Practice in Cost Sharing and Financing in Higher Education.* Manila: Department of External Relations, the Asian Development Bank.

Association of African Universities (AAU) (1997). *Revitalizing universities in Africa: Strategy and guidelines.* The World Bank.

Atuahene, F. (2009). Financing higher education through value added tax: A reveiew of the contribution of the Ghana Education Trust Fund (GETFund in fulfilment of the objectives of Act 581. *Journal of Higher Education in Africa,* 7(3), 29-60.

Bain, Olga. (2001). The Costs of Higher Education to Students and Parents in Russia: Tuition Policy Issues. *Peabody Journal of Education,* 76(3&4).

Best, J.W. & Khan, J. (2005). *Research in education 9th ed.* New Delhi: Prentice – Hall of India.

Bishop, G.(1989). *Alternative to education.* London: Macmillan.

Bloom, D. Canning, D., and Chan, K. (2005) *Higher Education and economic development in Africa.* Harvard University.

Burnham, G. M., Pariyo, G., Galiwango E. & Wabwire-Mangen, F. (2004). Discontinuation of cost sharing in Uganda. *Bulletin of the World Health Organization,* 82, 187-195.

Bollag B. (2004). *Improving tertiary education in Sub-Saharan Africa: Things that work.* Accra, Ghana.

Caillaud, F. et al. (2009). *Financing Tertiary Education in Africa.* UNESCO.

Carrol, Bidemi. (2004). *Dual Tuition Policy in Uganda.* Prepared for the International Comparative Higher Education Finance and Accessibility Project.

Chacha, N. C. (2002). *Public universities, private funding the challenges in East Africa.* A paper presented during the international symposium on African universities in the 21st century. University of Illinois

Chapman, B. (2005). *Income contingent loans for higher education: international reform.* Discussion paper no. 491. The Australian National University, Centre for Economic Policy Research. Retrieved on April 8, 2010 from http://dspace.anu.edu.au/bitstream/1885/43204/1/DP491.pdf

Council of Higher Education. (2001). Developing African Higher Education. South Africa: Council of Higher Education.

Court, D. (1999). *Financing Higher Education in Africa: Makerere, the Quit Revolution.* Hague: Centre for Higher Education Policy Studies (CHEPS).

Creswell, J.W (2009). *Research Design: qualitative, Quantitative and Mixed Methods Approaches.* 3rd ed. New Delhi SAGE.

Cronbach, L. J. (1990). *Essentials of Psychological Testing* (5th. Ed.). New York: Harper Collins Publisher.

CSA (2010). *Analytical report on the 2009 urban employment unemployment survey.* Statistical bulletin 477. Addis Ababa.

FDRE (2005). *A plan for Accelerate and Sustained Development to End Poverty* (PASDEP 2005/06 – 2009/10), Addis Ababa.

FDRE. (2002). *Income Tax Proclamation No. 286/2002.* Federal Negarit Gazeta, Addis Ababa: Berahn and Selam Printing Enterprise.

FDRE. (2003). *Higher Education Cost Sharing Council of Minsters Regulation No. 91/2003.* Federal Negarit Gazeta, Addis Ababa: Berahn and Selam Printing Enterprise.

FDRE. (2008). *Higher Education Cost Sharing Council of Minsters Regulation No. 154/2008*. Federal Negarit Gazeta, Addis Ababa: Berahn and Selam Printing Enterprise.

FDRE. (2009). *Higher Education Proclamation N0. 650/2009*. Federal Negarit Gazeta, Addis Ababa: Berahn and Selam Printing Enterprise.

Gay, L.R. & Airasian, P. (2000). *Educational Research: Competencies and application.* 6th ed. Columbus: Merrill.

Graduate School of Education's Center for Comparative and Global Studies in Education. (2009). *The International Comparative Higher Education Finance and Accessibility.* New York at Buffalo. Retrieved on June 28, 2010 from http://www.gse.buffalo.edu/org/IntHigherEdFinance.

International Comparative Higher Education Finance and Accessibility Project and University of Dar es Salaam. (2002). *Financing Higher Education in Eastern and Southern Africa: Diversifying Revenue and Expanding Accessibility.* Dar es Salaam, Tanzania March 24-28, 2002.

Ishengoma, M. J. (2004). Cost-Sharing in Higher Education in Tanzania: Fact or Fiction? *JHEA/RESA,* 2 (2). 101–133.

Johnstone, D. B. (2004a). Higher education finance and accessibility: Tuition fees and student loans in sub-Saharan Africa. *Journal of Higher Education in Africa*, 2(2):

Johnstone, D. B. (2004b), The Applicability of Income Contingent Loans in Developing and Transitional Countries, *Journal of Educational Planning and Administration,* 18(2), 159-174.

Johnstone, D. B. (2004c). The economics and politics of cost sharing in higher education: comparative perspectives. *Economics of Education Review*, 23, 403–410

Johnstone, D. B. and Marcucci, P. (2010). *Financing higher education worldwide: Who pays? Who should Pay?* Baltimore, Maryland: The Johns Hopkins University Press.

Kiamba, C. (2003). *The experience of privately sponsored studentship and other income generating activities at the University of Nairobi.* Paper prepared for the World Bank Regional Training Conference on Improving Tertiary Education in Sub-Saharan Africa: Accra, Ghana.

Kiamba, C. (2004). The Privately-Sponsored Students and Other Income-Generating Activities at the University of Nairobi. *Journal of Higher Education in Africa,* 2(2), pp. 53-74.

Marcucci, P. Johnstone, D. B. and Ngolovi, M. (2008). Higher Educational Cost-Sharing, Dual-Track Tuition Fees, and Higher Educational Access: The East African Experience. *Peabody Journal of Education,* 83(1), 101-116.

Marcucci, P. N. and Johnstone, D. B. (2007). Tuition fee policies in a comparative perspective: Theoretical and political rationales. *Journal of Higher Education Policy and Management*, 29 (1), 25–40.

Materu, P. (2006). *Re-visioning Africa's tertiary education in the transition to a knowledge economy.* Johannesburg: South Africa.

Mayanja, M. K. (1996). *The Social Background of Markerere University Students and the Potential for Cost Sharing.* Association of African Universities.

MOE (2010). *Education Sector Development Program IV (2010/11-2014/15).* Addis Ababa, Ethiopia.

MOE (2009). *Implementation guideline for cost sharing regulation No.154/2008.* Addis Ababa, Ethiopia.

MOE. (2005-2009). *Education Statistics Annual Abstracts.* Addis Ababa, Ethiopia.

MOE. (2005). *Education Sector Development Program III (ESDP-III).* Addis Ababa.

Mpiza, M. (2007). *The Impacts of Cost Sharing on Students in Public Universities in Tanzania: A case study of The University of Dar es Salaam.* MPhil theses, University of Oslo, Norway

Mugabushaka, A., Teichler, U., and Schomburg, H. (2003). Failed or self-hindering prophecies? Employment experiences of African graduates in 1990s. *Journal of Higher Education in Africa.* 1, (1), 57-77.

Mwinzi, Dinah (2002). *The Impact of Cost-Sharing Policy on the Living Conditions of Students in Kenyan Public Universities: The Case of Nairobi and MOI Universities.* Paper presented at the 28th Annual International Symposium Sponsored by Council for The Development of Social Science Research in Africa (CODESRIA), Dakar and Centre of African Studies University of Illinois.

Obasi, I. N. and Eboh E. C. (2002). *Cost Sharing Crises in Nigerian Universities: Policy Lessons from an Empirical Study.* An Essay Submitted to the Secretary-General, Association of African Universities under the 2nd Phase of the Programme of Research on Higher Education Policy and Management

Obasi, I.N. & Eboh, E.E. (2004). *The cost-sharing dilemma in Nigerian Universities: Empirical lessons for policy adjustments in African universities in the twenty first century.* Logon.

Otieno, W. (2004). *The Private Entry University Scheme in Kenya.* Presented at a Consultative Workshop on Dual Track Tuition in East Africa. International.

Otieno, W. (2005). *Dual Track Tuition in Kenya's Public Universities: A Study of the Circumstances and Conditions Under Which Student Attitudes Towards Cost Sharing Would Change.* Prepared for the International Comparative Higher Education Finance and Accessibility Project.

Population Reference Bureau (2009). *World Population data sheet.*

Saint W. (2004). Higher Education in Ethiopia: The Vision and Its Challenges. *Journal of Higher Education in Africa,* 2(3), .83–113.

Salerno C. (2006). Cost Sharing in Higher Education Financing: Economic Perils in Developing Countries. *International Higher Education,* Number 43.

Sawyers, A (2004). Challenges facing African Universities: Selected issues. *African Studies Review,* 47 (1), 1-59.

Schwarzenberger, A. and Opheim, V. (2009). Cost-Sharing in Higher Education: Differences between countries and between distinct socio-economic groups. *Tertiary Education and Management,* 15(2), 157–172.

Sodhi, T.S. (1984). *Education and Economic Development.* Delhi: Vikas.

Teshome Yizengaw (2003). *Transformations in Higher Education: Experiences with Reform and Expansion in Ethiopian Higher Education System.* Keynote paper prepared for a Regional Training Conference on Improving Tertiary Education in Sub-Saharan Africa: Things That Work, Accra, September 23-25, 2003.

Teshome Yizengaw. (2007). Implementation of Cost Sharing in the Ethiopian Higher Education Landscape: Critical Assessment and the Way Forward. *Higher Education Quarterly,* 61 (2), 171–196.

Teshome, Y (2006). Cost sharing in the Ethiopian higher education system: The need, implications and future directions. *The Ethiopian Journal of Higher Education.* 3 (2). 1-32.

Todaro, M. Smith, C.S. (2012). *Economic Development.* (11th ed.) New York: Long man.

Vandenberghe, V., and Debande, O. (2005). *Is Free Higher Education an Implicit Loan? An empirical assessment using Belgian, German & UK data.*

Wanna L. (2004). Cost sharing in higher education: the international experience and the lessons to be learned. *The Ethiopian Journal of Higher Education,* 1(2), 17-32.

World Bank. (2004). *Higher education development for Ethiopia: Pursuing the vision.* Washington, DC: World Bank.

World Bank (2008). *Ethiopia at a glance.* Retrieved November 6, 2010 from http://devdata.worldbank.org/AAG/eth_aag.pdf

World Bank. (2010). *Financing Higher Education in Africa.* Retrieved on Nov. 21, 2010 from http://siteresources.worldbank.org /EDUCATION/ Resources/ 278200-1099079877269/Financing_higher_edu_Africa.pdf

Wright, J. S. (2008). *An Investigation into the Equity and Efficiency of Australia's Higher Education System.* PhD thesis, School of Arts and Sciences, Australian Catholic University.

Annex 1:

Summary of Cost sharing Proclamation No.154/2008

Article 10 of the Regulation No. 154/2008 states the power and duties of the Ministry of Education as:

Without prejudice to other provisions in this Regulation, the Ministry shall have the following powers and duties:

1/ to oversee and ensure the implementation of this Regulation;
2/ to approve the amount apportioned by higher education institutions from the beneficiaries
3/ to issue, directives for the proper implementation of this Regulation.
4/ to determine on the content of contractual document;
5/ to issue specific directives on the areas and modalities of compulsory service in place of payment of the cost sharing.

Article 11 of the Regulation No. 154/2008 states the power and duties of the Ethiopian Revenues and Customs Authority as follows:

Without prejudice to other provisions of this Regulation, the Authority shall have the following powers and duties:

1/ to notify each beneficiary and employer the total amount of payment to be made by the beneficiary together with the monthly payment;
2/ to follow up, supervise and collect the total amount of payment to be made by the beneficiary;
3/ to create the necessary procedures and organizational structure for the implementation of the objective;
4/ to issue certificate of completion of payment for the beneficiary who fully discharges his obligations;
5/ to issue a Taxpayer Identification Number for each beneficiary;
6/ to facilitate for the collection of the graduate tax from beneficiaries employed in regional states;
7/ to delegate the power to collect cost sharing payments to regional and municipality finance bureaus;
8/ to undertake various promotional activities with a view to effectively collect cost-sharing payments.

Article 12 of the Regulation No. 154/2008 states powers and duties of institutions of higher learning as follows:

Without prejudice to other provisions in this Regulation, institutions of higher education shall have the following powers and duties to:

1/ follow up the implementation of the cost sharing system;

2/ notify the beneficiary, at the beginning of the academic year, the appropriate amount of cost the beneficiary has to share, and to keep record of all necessary data.

3/ provide the beneficiary with necessary information and documents related to the amounts of cost-sharing owned by them upon leaving the institutions.

4/ organize units responsible for matters relating to cost-sharing;

5/ collect advance payments from beneficiaries and transfer the same to the Ethiopian Revenues and Customs Authority;

6/ submit a list of graduates and those who discontinued, with disclosure of cost sharing amounts owed by each of them, to the relevant body at every academic year;

7/ keep original or temporary academic certificate (including the official) of beneficiaries with itself and ensure that related documents are not given to beneficiaries or any shared party until the beneficiaries have fulfilled their service obligation, or in respect of cash payment until the beneficiary paid total amount or present the necessary guarantee for the payment.

Article 13 of the Regulation No. 154/2008 again states the duties of the Ethiopian Revenues and Customs Authority, which should have been incorporated in Article 11. This article and the articles 14-18 are new articles added to Regulation No. 154/2008.

The Article of the Regulation No. 154/2008 states that:

The Ethiopian Revenues and Customs Authority have the following powers and duties to:

1/ develop a system and direct, supervise, and coordinate the implementation of payments of cost sharing of higher education; and

2/ issue directives with respect to collection of payments and matters related to thereto.

Article 14 states the powers and responsibilities of the bodies where compulsory services take place. This Article of the Regulation No. 154/2008 states that:

Pursuant to the directives issued by the Ministry (MoE) for the payment of graduate tax for other fields beneficiaries who are trained in Health and Education fields are expected to fulfil their obligation only by rendering services. The concerned bodies shall have the following power and responsibilities.

1. take the necessary steps that professionals trained in public higher education institutions are assigned to federal and regional institutions and render service for not more than their training period;

2. ensure beneficiaries who have pursued their studies at home fulfil their service obligations in accordance with the agreements they entered into; revoke their licenses they authorize them to practice in any field where they have failed to discharge their obligations; and issue directives for the implementation of the same;

3. follow up the cases of those professionals who have failed to discharge their service obligations and notify the Ministry of Education for the necessary legal action.

Article 17 is about duties to cooperate:

This article promulgates due to cooperate in the implementation of the regulation in two sub-articles.

1. Unless permitted otherwise by specific directive to be issued by the Ministry any government or private education institution shall not accept an applicant for the further higher training before ensuring that the applicant has fulfilled his service obligation or financial duty.

2. Every person shall have the duty to cooperate with the concerned authorities in the implementation of this Regulation.

The government also made it clear in Proclamation No. 154/2008 to the beneficiaries how the cost sharing works. This Proclamation among other things states that:

1. All beneficiaries of public institutions of higher learning shall share full costs related with boarding and lodging and minimum 15% of tuition related costs. The amount to be shared shall be calculated based on the cost to be incurred at each institution and programme of study and shall be revealed to the beneficiaries at the beginning of each academic year.

2. The beneficiary shall pursue his education after entering a written contract agreement with the respective institution for the discharge of the amount of cost to be borne.

3. Any beneficiary who discontinues or completes his education shall be given a document stating the amount owed. The document shall have full name of the beneficiary, address, photo and other relevant information.

4. The cost of education and training shall be revised at least every three years. The Ministry shall enact directives to this effect.

5. Only an Ethiopian national is eligible for pursuing his higher education or training upon the contractual commitment for future payment, in cash or in service, of his share of the cost in the form of graduate tax.

Notes about the Authors

Wanna Leka currently is Associate Professor and lectures at the Institute of Educational Research, Addis Ababa University. He obtained his PhD in the U.S.A. During 1992 – 1994 he worked as General Manager for the Educational Materials Production and Distribution Agency (EMPDA). He has also served as a consultant for the African Union Education Section and UNESCO/IICBA. Dr. Wanna has authored and co-authored a number of evaluation reports arising from his consultative work.

Desalegn Chalchisa currently is Assistant Professor at the Institute of Educational Research, Addis Ababa University. He obtained his PhD in India, from Andhra University. During 1981 – 1990 he worked as an instructor of Psychology at the Asmara Teachers Training Institute. He has also served as a consultant for Basic Education Overhaul System. He served also as a Director of the Institute of Educational Research, Addis Ababa University. Dr. Desalegn has authored and co-authored a number of evaluation reports arising from his consultative work.

www.ingramcontent.com/pod-product-compliance
Lightning Source LLC
Chambersburg PA
CBHW021716230426
43668CB00008B/851